AIRPOINTS GOLD ELITE

D0933755

VINEYARDS OF NEW ZEALAND COOKBOOK

VIKING

VIKING An imprint of Penguin Books

Penguin Books (NZ) Ltd,
cnr Rosedale and Airborne Roads, Albany,
Auckland 1310, New Zealand
Penguin Books Ltd,
27 Wrights Lane, London W8 5TZ, England
Penguin Putnam Inc, 375 Hudson Street,
New York, NY 10014, United States
Penguin Books Australia Ltd, 487 Maroondah
Highway, Ringwood, Australia 3134
Penguin Books Canada Ltd, 10 Alcorn Avenue,
Toronto, Ontario, Canada M4V 3B2
Penguin Books (South Africa) Pty Ltd,
5 Watkins Street, Denver Ext 4, 2094, South Africa
Penguin Books India (P) Ltd,
11, Community Centre, Panchsheel Park,
New Delhi 110 017, India
Penguin Books Ltd, Registered Offices:
Harmondsworth, Middlesex, England

First published by Penguin Books (NZ) Ltd, 2001

1 3 5 7 9 10 8 6 4 2

Produced by Chanel Publishers Ltd
Designed and typeset by Athena Sommerfeld
Printed by Bookbuilders, Hong Kong
ISBN 0 670 91110 0

www.penguin.co.nz

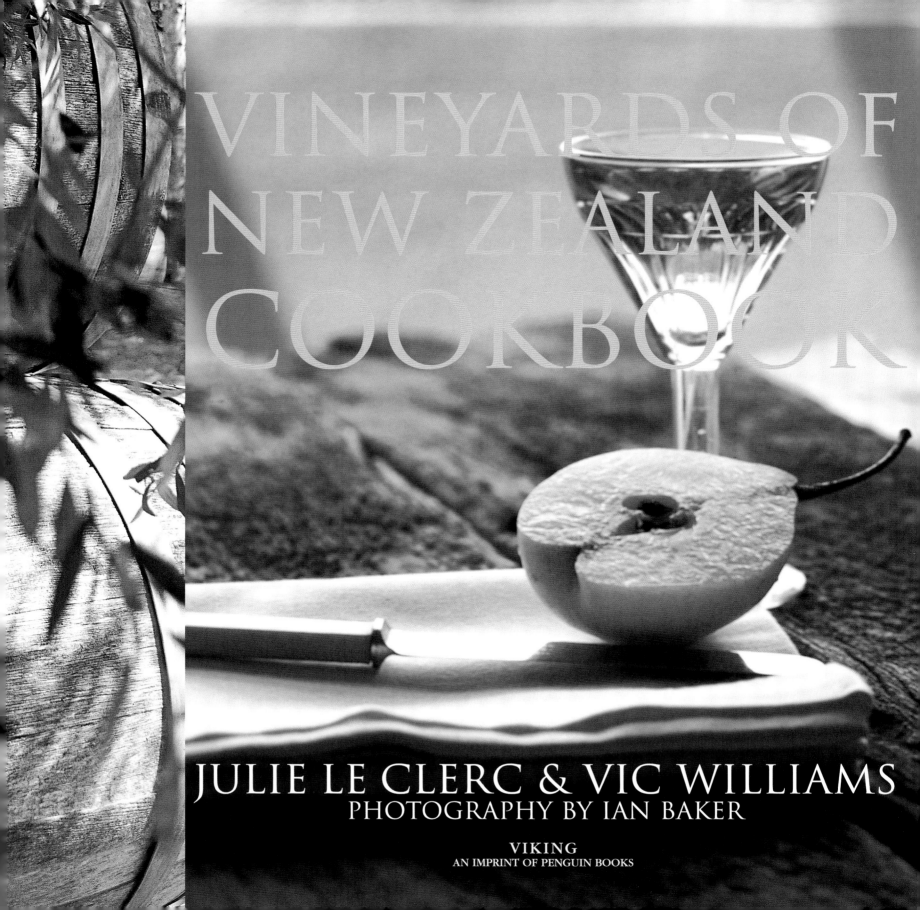

VINEYARDS OF NEW ZEALAND COOKBOOK

JULIE LE CLERC & VIC WILLIAMS
PHOTOGRAPHY BY IAN BAKER

VIKING
AN IMPRINT OF PENGUIN BOOKS

ACKNOWLEDGEMENTS

Passion is a unifying trait that seems,
in my view, to be a character prerequisite
of vintners and chefs. To the people of the
vineyards and their kitchens, thanks for
collaborating on this project and for giving
so generously of your time and expertise.
The list of contributing vineyards is limited
only by the number of pages available in
this volume.

Sabato Ltd generously supplied specialist
ingredients appearing in these recipes.
For enquiries phone 09 630 8751 or visit
www.sabato.co.nz

Many thanks to Gourmet Direct for
providing premium quality game, meat
and poultry. For enquiries phone 0800
737 800 or visit www.gourmetdirect.com

Grateful thanks to Country Road
Homeware for contributing beautiful
dinnerware for photographic use.
For enquiries phone 0800 105 655.

Copperware kindly lent by St Clair.
For enquiries phone 0800 226 659. **JLeC**

This book would not have been possible
without Bernice Beachman, publisher at
Penguin Books, who deserves full credit
as the inspiration behind this remarkable
work. We thank Philippa Gerrard for her
unfailing dedication to excellent production,
and Athena Sommerfeld for her brilliant,
compelling design bringing all our efforts
together. It was a joy to work with such
an outstanding team whose verve and
professionalism permeate these pages.

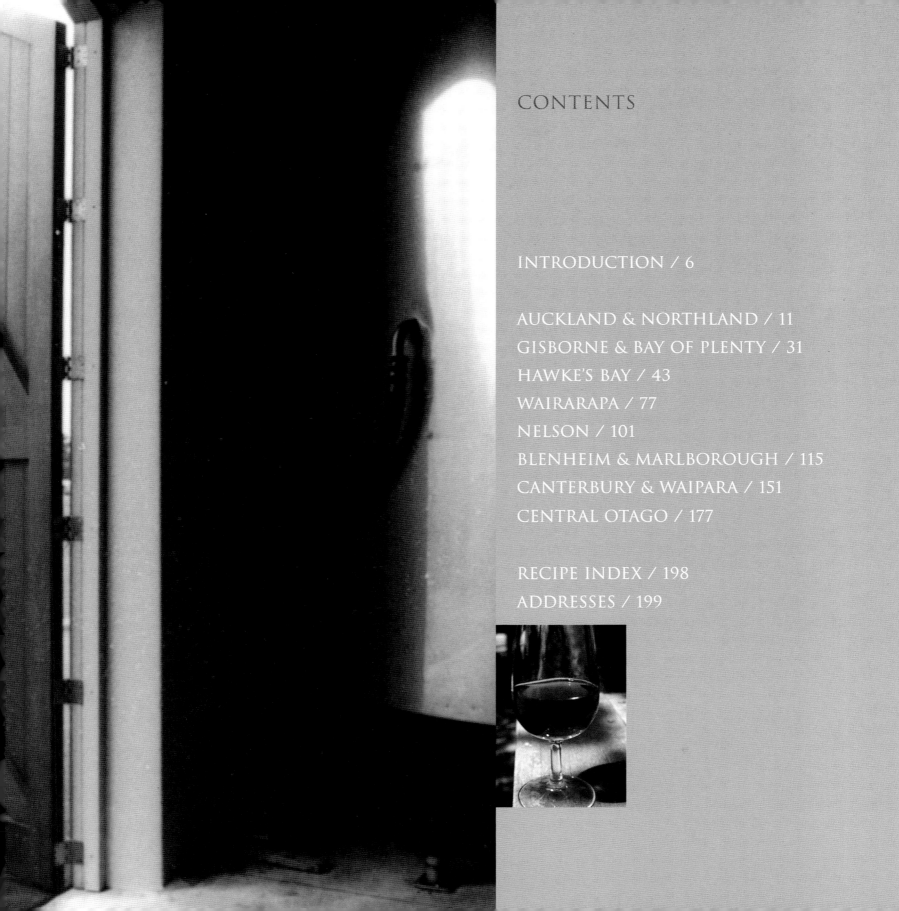

CONTENTS

Anticipate a magical culinary and vinous experience. Journey our land, it is being transformed, and it is hard to imagine a more dynamic and evolving scene or more breathtaking countryside or more generous, spirited people. I feel privileged to have met the custodians of mesmerising vines, and passionate makers of wine and food.

This book was a great opportunity for chefs to display recipes from their personal repertoires. They live and work in terrain that is inspiring, and their food expresses this. Local produce is chosen to honour the seasons, and therefore harvest its full goodness. The chefs embraced the book's style, donating recipes that capture the feeling of the land and the wine. Unrestrained ideas flowed onto plates. I, too, took inspiration from the regional variations of wine and produce in the creation of my own featured dishes. Rapport should exist between the region, the wine and the dish in order to appreciate their true connections.

The recipes in this book are partners to wines rather than complicated combinations. The beauty of this concept is that the dishes were devised with the wine in mind, and not the other way round. To the best of my ability, I sought to present original dishes to connect with the characters, taste and texture, depth and weight of each wine. Of course, some variation occurs from vintage to vintage, as the wines age, and to some degree with individual palates. In essence, the pairings are of this moment in time, though that is not to say such partnerships won't work in a year or even ten, just that there will be subtle differences. Slight alterations may need to be made to accommodate vintage or cellaring variations in the wines or according to personal taste. For example, with age a ginger note may become more predominant in a cool climate riesling. Alter the amount of ginger or spice in the recipe if this pleases you. In some instances, your taste buds may not agree with mine. Taste for yourself.

It has been my pleasure to collaborate with Vic Williams and Ian Baker on this project. Vic has added a wine writer's perspective through his expansive knowledge and enthusiasm. With photographic expertise and good humour, Ian has beautifully captured our compelling adventure on film.

I miss being surrounded by vines, well tended and prolific. And the intimate experience of sharing wine with its creator, wine so full of character that it tastes of the winemaker's personality, and has a texture reflecting the significance of the region where it is grown. Wine to enjoy with food. For wine with food gives eating shape and rhythm, and a sense of ritual to even the most uncomplicated or spontaneous of meals.

Simple, gutsy food is the best food in the world. It tastes superior and communicates more meaning than any fancily formed dish or jumble of bewildering tastes. That is why I strive to create good, clean flavour combinations that gratify the appetite in a direct and nurturing way.

The dishes here are very much of New Zealand, with a slight leaning to the Mediterranean. We can learn much from the people of that warm region who find it natural, sensible and delicious to spend long unhurried hours at the table, even when there is no special occasion. Combining food and wine and an appealing setting achieves a harmony that is pleasing to all the senses. So I encourage you to recreate the tastes of each vineyard. Whether you take the journey by land or through the pages of this book, it will be memorable. **Julie Le Clerc**

We have come a long way.

Not too many decades ago, wine was something that came out only at Christmas, often in the form of some mysterious bottle that had been lurking in the back of a kitchen cupboard since the same time the year before.

Now, this most sophisticated of beverages is assuming its rightful place in an increasing number of New Zealand homes.

The wowsers would have it that wine is 'just another drink', but they are wrong. Wine is designed to be enjoyed – in moderation, of course – as part of our everyday meals. The alcohol it contains is simply a by-product of the metamorphosis that transforms ripe grapes into one of the most magical substances on earth.

Matching specific wines with individual dishes is something of a New World phenomenon. In the traditional winemaking countries of Europe, little thought is put into partnering the flavours in the glass with those on the plate because the wine of the region has always gone with food from the local fields. Inevitably, they work well together, but it is more a matter of tradition than careful planning.

In our part of the world, we can choose wine from anywhere in the country. But if the food comes from the same region – Marlborough sauvignon blanc with Greenshell mussels from the nearby Sounds, for example – the match will take on extra meaning. That is the ethos of this book.

Touring the vineyards of New Zealand is a hugely pleasurable experience, and that pleasure is enhanced by the number of cafés and restaurants either attached to the wineries, or situated close enough to promote local wines with pride.

Julie Le Clerc's food is perfect with the honest flavours of New Zealand wine. Great wine is made in the vineyard – the less the winemaker has to do to capture the straightforward flavours of the land in the bottle, the better the final product will be. Julie adopts a similar philosophy in the kitchen. Her food is honest and direct, and it accurately reflects the region that gave her the ingredients.

Some of the dishes in this book were devised by Julie after she had tasted a particular wine; others were developed by chefs or winemakers keen to find the perfect match for their products. Often, Julie worked with them to finalise the flavours she wanted on the plate. Ian Baker's splendid photographs capture the essence of those flavours. My role was to background not only the featured wine, but also the other stars in each winery's portfolio.

Of course, we have barely scratched the surface. There are nearly 400 wine companies in New Zealand, and profiling them all would have meant publishing a book of Tolstoyan proportions.

Inevitably, many places we would have liked to spotlight missed final selection. But you, dear reader, can fill in the gaps. Put a week or two aside sometime in the not-too-distant future, and travel around as many winemaking regions as you can. The scene is constantly changing, and you are sure to discover many delights that have so far remained unheralded. Life can hold few greater pleasures. **Vic Williams**

NEW ZEALAND
WINE REGIONS

NORTHLAND

MATAKANA
AUCKLAND ● ● WAIHEKE IS.

BAY OF PLENTY
HAMILTON ● ● TAURANGA

WAIKATO   GISBORNE

GISBORNE ●

NAPIER ●
HAWKE'S BAY

NELSON   WAIRARAPA
                                 MARTINBOROUGH
NELSON ●   ● WELLINGTON
        BLENHEIM ●

MARLBOROUGH

WAIPARA ●

CHRISTCHURCH ●

CANTERBURY

QUEENSTOWN ●

CENTRAL OTAGO

● DUNEDIN

Matakana Estate

AUCKLAND & NORTHLAND

IS WHERE IT ALL BEGAN FOR SOME OF NEW ZEALAND'S BEST-KNOWN WINE COMPANIES.

PIONEERS LIKE JOSIP BABICH and Marino Selak arrived in this country from Dalmatia in the early 1900s, and headed up north to dig gum out of the kauri swamps. It was back-breaking work, but it enabled them to save enough to buy land. It was on these plots, often in the hillsides to the west of rapidly growing Auckland city, that they planted grapes.

Most of those original vines have long gone, and the few that remain are surrounded by spreading suburbia. But the area is steeped in vinous history. Pleasant Valley, Soljans, Nobilo, West Brook, Collard Brothers, Landmark Estate, Mazuran's and Pacific are among the many other establishments that can trace their origins back 70 years or more.

West Auckland remained the vinous centre for the top third of the North Island for many years, but in the new millennium other regions are vying for the title.

Waiheke Island, a short ferry ride from the mainland, has captured the enthusiast's imagination with a series of startlingly good reds based on the so-called Bordeaux varieties, cabernet sauvignon, merlot and cabernet franc.

An easy drive north of the city, Matakana is still sorting out which varieties are best suited to its sunny, maritime climate. Early indications are that pinot gris will be the local jewel in the crown, but excellent chardonnay, merlot and even a couple of Italian styles have all been produced in the last few vintages. David Hoskins and Mary Evans, at Heron's Flight, were early pioneers, and produce an always-interesting range of wines that sell mainly at their pleasant café, but there are many other properties worth visiting.

Right at the top of the North Island, Monty Knight defied the sceptics by planting grapes on a site overlooking Ninety Mile Beach. His Okahu Estate wines have achieved good show success, and command a loyal

Mudbrick Vineyard

following. Monty had the area to himself for many years, but now there is a growing trickle of vineyards between his picturesque site and Mario and Barbara Vuletich's Longview Estate, a landmark property adjoining the main highway a couple of hours to the south.

Head in the other direction from Auckland, and you will find another vinous outcrop at Clevedon. Here, fine food enthusiasts Enzio and Margaret Bettio are making Italian-style wines unlike anything produced in New Zealand before, retired District Court judge Ken Mason and his wife, Diane, produce a handful of impressive reds, and radio talk-back host Leighton Smith is determined to prove his favourite grape, shiraz (syrah), is perfect for the local climate. Other properties are springing up on a regular basis.

In the Waikato, Tom van Dam produces his colourfully labelled Rongopai range at the former Te Kauwhata government viticultural research station, and Mark Compton at Mangatawhiri puts together the respected De Redcliffe portfolio. Across the country, Peter Stiffe and Catherine Young fly the flag for the steel town of Waiuku.

Obviously, climate and soil types vary tremendously between Northland and the Waikato – even Kumeu and Henderson, only a few kilometres apart in West Auckland, produce wines that are quite different from one another. The variation means there is no obvious list of ideal varieties for this spread-out region. Cabernet sauvignon, for example, performs well on Waiheke Island, but struggles to ripen in Henderson on all but the most sun-drenched sites.

But wine industry people are a versatile lot. Other regions like Marlborough and Central Otago might have the limelight at present, but Auckland and the areas north and south of it will always have a major contribution to make to the country's vinous jigsaw. **VW**

Matakana Estate

Matakana Estate is a boutique-sized vineyard commanding a unique and picturesque position. A seat in the dedicated wine-tasting facility with a view over the carefully nurtured vines provides an idyllic environment to sample their range, presented for tasting with a small handbook of evocative and informative wine notes.

The passion of the family team is evident in the whole operation. It is easy to see why they chose this site to realise their dream of producing wines that, to quote their brochure, 'embody quality without compromise'.

Matakana's red blends are made using traditional Bordeaux methods. Each grape variety is matured separately, then the highest quality barrels are blended by the winemaker to create the best possible blend for the vintage. **JLeC**

Sage Crusted Lamb Rack with Wild Forest Mushroom Gravy

SERVES 4

3/4 cup dried forest mushrooms, or 1 1/2 cups sliced fresh specialty mushrooms

2 tblsp Dijon mustard

6 thick slices mixed grain bread, crusts removed

2 tblsp chopped fresh sage

1 egg, beaten

sea salt and freshly ground black pepper

4 lamb French racks, trimmed

1/4 cup sherry vinegar

1 cup meat glaze (reduced beef or venison stock)

1 Cover dried mushrooms with warm water and leave to soak for 1/2 hour then drain well. Spread Dijon mustard over meat.

2 Process bread into crumbs and mix with sage and egg. Season with salt and pepper and press onto outside of lamb. Place racks into an oven pan.

3 Roast in an oven preheated to 190°C for 15–20 minutes for medium rare. Remove to rest and keep warm while preparing the gravy.

4 Heat sherry vinegar in a pan until reduced to a tablespoonful. Add the beef or venison stock to heat through, simmer to reduce to a sauce consistency if necessary. Add drained mushrooms and adjust seasoning with salt and pepper to taste.

5 Slice lamb racks and serve with wild mushroom gravy.

Recipe created by Julie Le Clerc

Wine: Matakana Estate Merlot/Cabernet Sauvignon/Franc/Malbec

This blend (in 1999, 37% merlot, 22% cabernet sauvignon, 21% cabernet franc and 20% malbec) is a good advertisement for the region. Merlot's plum and leather notes are evident in the bouquet, and tie in nicely with the natural sweetness of the lamb. The sage accentuates the mintiness of the cabernet sauvignon and its more floral cousin, cabernet franc, while the earthy notes of malbec are perfect with the rustic wild mushroom sauce.

Matakana Estate has made a very good impression in a short time. An exceptionally good pinot gris heads the white portfolio, joining an elegant chardonnay and an outspoken sémillon.

The blend is the red wine flagship, but a straight syrah also shows great promise for the future of the variety in this region. **VW**

HERON'S FLIGHT

A family of herons breed in the nearby estuary entrance; their flights over the vineyard have inspired the name. Heron's Flight is a very friendly establishment. A farmhouse-style atmosphere prevails here, with the ethos that the kitchen is central to life. The menu combines delicious flavours using fresh ingredients from Heron's Flight's own estate and local suppliers.

The café's covered terrace is a restful place to shelter from the glittering sunshine and gaze dreamily over the prolific garden towards the vines. Sit and rest a while, enjoy the food, fine wine and company, for at Heron's Flight they operate in the belief that wine is best appreciated when combined with the tantalising mix of food, friends and a convivial environment.

Heron's Flight grow as much as they can on site, fruit and vegetables, herbs, pretty sunflowers and lavender, and even make their own vinegar and verjuice from an ancient recipe. They enjoy promoting food artisans within the region by purveying their products, which include extra virgin olive oil, mustard made with wine, chutneys and locally roasted organic coffee. **JLeC**

Matakana pioneers David Hoskins and Mary Evans are firm believers that the best way to enjoy wine is with honest food, ideally in the company of good friends. It is an admirable philosophy that is encapsulated in their small portfolio. These are wines for hedonists – they are definitely not intended to be analysed in the hallowed surroundings of some dedicated tasting facility. David is an experimenter, and while he would be the first to admit that not everything he tries works, his wines are well worth a search. Look for approachable chardonnay and a superbly packaged red made from sangiovese, an Italian variety that is very rare in this country. **VW**

Vine-Barbequed Baby Squid stuffed with Prawns & Basil

SERVES 4

300g raw prawn meat, veins removed

300g white fish fillets, cubed

finely grated zest and juice of 1 lemon

1/2 cup cream

1/4 cup fresh basil leaves, chopped

2 tblsp extra virgin olive oil

sea salt and freshly ground black pepper

650g baby squid tubes, cleaned

toothpicks

extra lemons, halved

1 Place prawn meat and fish into the bowl of a food processor and pulse to roughly chop. Add lemon zest and juice and cream. Process to form a textured paste. Remove to a bowl and mix in chopped basil, oil, salt and pepper to taste.

2 Half fill squid tubes with prawn mixture and thread toothpicks over openings to secure. Do not overfill squid or mixture will burst out during cooking.

3 Gently cook stuffed squid tubes and lemon halves over a preheated barbecue or grill for 2 minutes on each side, or until filling is just cooked through but still moist.

4 Slice squid in half to serve with grilled lemon halves.

Recipe created by Julie Le Clerc

Wine: Kumeu River Chardonnay

The Brajkovich family has an international reputation for high-quality chardonnay – in the US this member of the portfolio is known simply as 'the great New Zealand white'. Michael matures it in French oak barrels, and allows it to go through a full malolactic fermentation, a natural process that converts sharp malic acids (think Granny Smith apples) to softer lactic acids (think milk). As a result, it has a creamy texture that perfectly matches the squid's fish and prawn filling. Chardonnay's citric notes are picked up by the lemon zest, and the spiciness of French oak sits well with the basil.

Kumeu River Chardonnay and the slightly pricier Mate's Vineyard Chardonnay, made from grapes grown on a single site across the road from the winery, are the best-known wines in the portfolio, but the family also produces an impressive pinot gris and a small range of reds, including a pinot noir that shows the bottom half of the country doesn't have exclusive rights to this finicky variety. **VW**

Kumeu River

Kumeu is made up of striking countryside, where fruit orchards give way to land lush with rows of vines. The first Kumeu River grapes were crushed in 1944 by the late Mate Brajkovich. The family patriarch did a huge amount to promote New Zealand wine around the world, and his presence can still be felt throughout the winery and vineyard, run today by Melba Brajkovich and her three sons, Paul, Milan and Michael, a Master of Wine.

A great food discovery is that uprooted sauvignon vines provide perfect barbecue fuel, burning down to add a distinctive vine-smoked flavour to any food. It was Mate Brajkovich who created the family's ingenious backyard barbecue. A nifty attachment that once graced a rotary clothesline lowers the cooking grate towards the embers, allowing food to cook perfectly without blackening. This delicate method of smoke infusion left the stuffed squid lusciously juicy and flavoursome. **JLeC**

Venison Medallions with a Sweet Potato & Apple Rosti & Berry Jus

SERVES 4

1 large kumara (sweet potato), peeled and grated

1 apple, peeled and grated

1 egg

sea salt and freshly ground black pepper

1/4 cup blackcurrant purée

1 cup meat glaze (reduced venison or beef stock)

olive oil

600g Cervena/venison tenderloin, cut into medallions

200g baby spinach

1/4 cup cream

freshly grated nutmeg

1   To make the rosti, combine grated kumara, apple and egg, season with salt and pepper to taste. Form into four patties and fry in a little olive oil, turning once until golden brown on both sides. Keep warm.

2   To make the berry jus, place blackcurrant purée and stock together in a saucepan. Bring to the boil then simmer until reduced by half.

3   Heat a pan with a little olive oil and cook seasoned venison medallions for 1–2 minutes on each side. Remove to rest for 5 minutes.

4   Wilt spinach in a hot pan with a little olive oil. Add cream to heat through and season with nutmeg, salt and pepper.

5   Place rosti on plates, top with spinach and venison. Spoon over berry jus.

Recipe created by chef Carston Blutner, Mudbrick Restaurant

Wine: Mudbrick Vineyard Church Bay Malbec

Malbec is a rustic, earthy grape that is perfectly suited to game dishes like Cervena/venison, ostrich or hare. It is not common in New Zealand, and what little we do grow is usually blended with other varieties like cabernet sauvignon and merlot. The 1999 Mudbrick reading of the style has blackcurrant and plum characters that are nicely picked up by the sauce. The grape's natural sweetness matches the kumara in the rosti. Naturally enough, much of Mudbrick's production is sold through the adjacent restaurant, so the label can be hard to find. The emphasis is on reds based on merlot and cabernet sauvignon, with syrah also making an appearance, but a middleweight chardonnay has a strong local following. **VW**

Mudbrick Vineyard

Sitting on a bluff five minutes from the Waiheke ferry terminal, the Mudbrick Restaurant and Winery commands spectacular views back to Auckland city across the Hauraki Gulf. The buildings are made from hand-hewn mud bricks, giving them a subtle and timeless style. Immaculate landscaping surrounds the buildings, and a pretty potager garden is well tended to supply the restaurant kitchen.

The Mudbrick Restaurant menu features elegant, well-executed food and a good selection of worthy New Zealand wines – the only compelling distraction from such excellent fare is that breathtaking view.

The Mudbrick winery is a semi-underground structure, once again built from earth bricks to help maintain a constant cellar temperature. The first vintage was harvested in 1996 and the vineyard's owners say their range is still evolving, with some varieties yet to come on stream. **JLeC**

Goldwater Estate

The Goldwaters pioneered winemaking on stunningly beautiful Waiheke Island, in Auckland's sparkling Hauraki Gulf. Their passion, combined with Waiheke Island's high sunshine hours, low summer rainfall and free-draining soil, provide the background for their outstanding portfolio.

A fine wine trail can be followed around the island, and Goldwater Estate is an important port of call. Winery tastings are available at the vineyard over the summer, and wines can be purchased (while stocks last!). While there is no restaurant on site, irresistible platters of fine cheeses and smoked meats can be ordered to accompany the nicely focused wines. It is possible to lose track of time while spending companionable hours at this beautiful spot surrounded by the vines and the goodwill of the people. **JLeC**

Raw Marinated Local Snapper with Lime Aioli

SERVES 4 AS AN ENTRÉE

400g snapper fillets, bones removed
1/2 cup fresh lime or lemon juice
250g fresh asparagus, trimmed
1/4 cup extra virgin olive oil
1 clove garlic, crushed
1 each red and yellow peppers, seeds removed and finely diced
sea salt and freshly ground black pepper
bed of fancy lettuce leaves
lemon or lime wedges to serve

LIME AIOLI:

2 egg yolks
4 cloves garlic, peeled and crushed
juice of 3 limes

sea salt
1/2 cup light-flavoured olive oil

1 Cut fish fillets into 2cm cubes and cover with lime or lemon juice. Leave to marinate for 1 hour.
2 Blanch asparagus tips in boiling salted water for 1 minute. Drain and refresh in ice-cold water.
3 Drain snapper, discarding juice, and toss with oil, crushed garlic and red and yellow peppers. Season with salt and pepper to taste.
4 To make lime aioli, whisk egg yolks, garlic and lime juice together with a little salt until pale and fluffy. Slowly drizzle in olive oil while whisking continuously until thick and creamy.
5 Arrange fish mixture and asparagus onto a bed of fancy lettuce leaves. Serve with lemon or lime wedges and aioli.

Recipe created by Jeanette Goldwater

Wine: Dog Point Marlborough Sauvignon Blanc

The Goldwaters are best known for an excellent Bordeaux-style red blend using their own grapes, but have been innovative in producing a couple of Marlborough wines, made with the help of regular flights to the South Island and many telephone calls from Kim. Marlborough sauvignon blanc is famous for its 'zing', a quality that is perfectly suited to the upfront flavours of citrus-marinated fish. Asparagus is listed in some old recipe books as an impossible match for wine – but the authors hadn't tried our sauvignon. It's perfect! **VW**

Goldwater Estate

Mudbrick Vineyard

Stonyridge Vineyard

STONYRIDGE WAIHEKE ISLAND

MATUA VALLEY WINERY & THE HUNTING LODGE

An attractive rural scene north-west of Auckland is home to Matua Valley Winery and the adjacent traditional villa that houses The Hunting Lodge restaurant.

The professional team at The Hunting Lodge work with the winery and together put much thought into both recipe creation and wine partnerships. The kitchen takes advantage of quality vegetables grown in the surrounding countryside, and organic produce is used whenever possible. Vine-ripened tomatoes with saturated flavour and delicate green beans are gathered from small-production local growers. Hand-picked herbs are plucked daily from the kitchen garden. Even macadamia nuts and specialty mushrooms are grown in the greater Auckland area. **JLeC**

SPICY BEEF FILLET WITH CURRANT COUSCOUS & NEEDLE MUSHROOMS

SERVES 4

1 cup chicken or vegetable stock or orange juice
1 tsp each cinnamon, cumin, cayenne pepper
1 cup couscous
2 tblsp currants
30g butter
100g needle mushrooms
800g premium beef tenderloin eye fillet, sliced into 12
2 tblsp chopped fresh mint
1/2 cup macadamia nuts, lightly toasted
sea salt

1 Bring the stock to the boil. Mix spices together and place half in a bowl with the couscous and currants. Pour over the boiling stock, cover with plastic wrap and leave to swell.

2 Heat a pan, add butter to melt, toss mushrooms in butter and cook gently. Season with a little salt.

3 Heat a char-grill pan, barbecue or grill. Lightly dust beef with remaining spices and a little salt. Cook beef quickly, turning once.

4 Tear the mint leaves by hand into small pieces. Fluff up couscous with a fork and toss through torn mint and toasted macadamia nuts. Season with salt to taste.

5 Arrange couscous then beef on a platter and scatter with needle mushrooms.

Recipe created by chef Geoffrey Scott, The Hunting Lodge

WINE: MATUA VALLEY MATHESON VINEYARD CABERNET/ MERLOT

The Hunting Lodge kitchen team chose this dish for the 1999 cabernet/merlot. They feel that the currants pick up and run with the berry flavours in the wine, the spices mingle with the caramelised sugars in the beef and play beautifully beside the smooth, spicy and very approachable characters of the wine.

Matua Valley produces a large range of wines, all of which enjoy a good reputation. The company's Ross and Bill Spence have pioneered several varieties in this country, including sauvignon blanc. A straight grenache – exceedingly rare in New Zealand – commands a loyal following. Matua Valley sauvignon is invariably of good quality, but impressive wines are also made from chardonnay and the red quartet of merlot, cabernet sauvignon, cabernet franc and malbec. **VW**

STONYRIDGE VINEYARD

It is easy to feel transported to some Mediterranean locale while relaxing on the sun-drenched outdoor terrace at Stonyridge Vineyard. The maritime climate, style and colours of the buildings, the grounds studded with twisted olive trees and the radiating rows of grapevines heighten this perception. Stonyridge even boasts the oldest commercial olive grove in New Zealand.

Grand tasting platters and creatively flavoursome meals can be enjoyed in a pleasantly informal atmosphere, along with selections from the carefully thought out wine list. Wine tastings and tours are conducted all year round. **JLeC**

ROASTED TOMATO & FETA TARTS

SERVES 6

1 carrot, peeled and sliced thinly
2 courgettes, trimmed and sliced thinly
1 each red, green and yellow peppers, sliced thinly
1 red onion, peeled and sliced thinly
2 tsp sweet La Chinata Spanish smoked paprika
2 tblsp quality balsamic vinegar
1 tblsp brown sugar
1 tblsp extra virgin olive oil
sea salt and freshly ground black pepper
8–10 small tomatoes, cores removed, cut into 8 wedges each
200g savoury short crust pastry
100g feta, cut into 1cm cubes

1 Pre-heat oven to 190°C. Place prepared vegetables, except tomatoes into a roasting pan and sprinkle with smoked paprika, balsamic vinegar, brown sugar, olive oil, salt and pepper. Roast for 20–30 minutes until caramelised. Roast tomatoes separately for 10 minutes.
2 Roll out pastry to 4mm thick and use to line six 8cm deep, fluted, loose-based tart shells. Prick with a fork and line with foil, fill with baking beans and bake blind for 15 minutes. Remove foil and baking beans. When cool transfer tart shells from tins to a baking tray.
3 Fill pastry cases with vegetables followed by feta and roasted tomatoes.
4 Place in hot oven and warm through for 5 minutes to serve.

Recipe created by chef Russell Wilson, Stonyridge Vineyard

WINE: STONYRIDGE LAROSE

Stephen White's famous red, a blend of cabernet sauvignon, merlot, cabernet franc, malbec and petit verdot, enjoys legendary status in New Zealand and quite a few other countries. Each release sells out within days, and the wines often reappear at auction, where they have been known to sell for several times their original price. The 1999 Larose is a powerful wine, but it boasts a measure of elegance that makes it a good match for a surprisingly large range of foods. Russell Wilson's tarts work well because the peppers tie in with the cabernet sauvignon in the blend – the grape is, after all, a distant cousin of sauvignon blanc, which has flavours often compared to peppers. The balsamic vinegar, aged for many years in oak casks, echoes the oak used for the wine's maturation, and the roasted tomatoes and red onions match the sweetness of the grapes. **VW**

NOT LONG AGO, MORE GRAPES WERE GROWN IN GISBORNE THAN ANYWHERE ELSE IN NEW ZEALAND.

Millton Vineyard

NOWADAYS, MARLBOROUGH occupies the top slot, but Gisborne is still the region where the big-name producers buy bulk juice.

But this coastal province has a dual personality. Signs on the roads leading into the township proclaim it as the chardonnay capital of New Zealand, and with more than half the vineyards devoted to this classic variety it is a reasonable description.

It could have been the country's oldest winemaking area. Marist missionaries landed there in the mid-1800s, but it was a mistake – they were actually heading for Hawke's Bay. They moved on and eventually founded Mission Estate, which now lays claim to being the oldest winemaking establishment still under its original ownership.

For years, müller-thurgau was the grape of choice for many Gisborne growers, but in the new millennium this big-cropping variety has fallen from favour. Now, quality-conscious vineyard owners coax all the flavour they can from a range of classic grapes.

It is largely white wine country. Cabernet sauvignon has always struggled to ripen, and most local examples are spoiled by green, herbal flavours. Merlot is more successful, but pinot noir is the new hope for the future, although few examples have been produced so far.

Because the region acts as the major vineyard area for the big names of the industry but has only a handful of vineyards of its own, Gisborne has often struggled to achieve the recognition it deserves. Yet it has produced many award-winning wines, most notably a series of chardonnays wearing the Villa Maria Reserve label.

And those who have chosen to set up in the province are among the most dedicated in the land.

Solicitor Ross Revington makes just two wines, an elegant chardonnay and a super-aromatic gewürztraminer. His production is tiny, but he has a keen following.

Local personalities the Thorpe brothers produce wine under a number of different labels, and at various times have been involved with a series of cafés, restaurants, tasting facilities and a cheese-making plant. Noel Amor and Alison Bendall's Amor-Bendall Wines is the newest name in town, and its first releases show a lot of promise. Self-confessed eccentric Phil Parker specialises in sparkling wine, but also makes the world's first wine each year under the label First Light Red.

We highlight just two Gisborne producers in this chapter – James and Annie Millton, because they have succeeded in making top-quality wine despite eschewing methods with which they philosophically disagree, and Denis Irwin, because he is a local pioneer and a New Zealand winemaking legend who has steadfastly refused to follow the rules.

Also included in this chapter are two Bay of Plenty wineries, Mills Reef and Morton Estate. Neither takes grapes from the area that hosts their wineries, but both have made a solid contribution to our country's wine industry. **VW**

Millton Vineyard

Pleasurable hours pass all too quickly with the Milltons at their beautiful Gisborne property. The Millton Vineyard is a small, family estate producing a selection of quality-focused wines harvested from their own organic vineyards, where they employ biodynamic viticultural techniques.

James Millton enjoys the challenge of growing and making chenin blanc in the traditional French way and talks of adding a degree of corruption into the wine, which he feels offers the wine personality and memory. And Millton wines are very memorable! The Milltons want to bring chenin blanc forward as a food wine. It is a unique variety with an array of jewel-like fruit characters that work particularly well with French Loire-style foods, hence the combination of Puy lentils and fennel bulb plus lemon thyme from Annie's herb garden.

Note: Purely for interest, James is experimenting with the alchemy of vinegar production and has come up with a brilliant caramelised version. It has a vivacious flavour reminiscent of great Spanish sherry vinegar, creating huge possibilities from a cook's point of view! **JLeC**

Lentil and fennel salad with lemon thyme

SERVES 4

1 cup Sabarot Puy lentils (high quality, fast cooking, French green lentils)
1 bay leaf
1 clove garlic, crushed
4 tblsp lemon-infused olive oil
3 tblsp Spanish sherry vinegar (look for Romulo, it has great flavour)
2 small fresh fennel bulbs, trimmed
2 cups baby spinach leaves
sea salt and freshly ground black pepper
sprigs of lemon thyme
lemon wedges to serve

1   Place lentils and bay leaf into a saucepan and cover with plenty of cold water. Bring to the boil then simmer for 20 minutes or until lentils are tender. Drain well. Toss with garlic, lemon-infused olive oil and sherry vinegar and leave to cool.
2   Cut fennel bulbs in half then slice thinly, avoiding the hard core. Blanch or even better still, bake with a little olive oil, salt and pepper, covered for 20 minutes at 180°C.
3   Toss cold lentils with spinach and prepared fennel. Season with salt and pepper to taste.
4   Serve scattered with lemon thyme and extra lemon wedges to squeeze over if desired.

Recipe created by Julie Le Clerc, inspired by Annie Millton

Wine: Millton Gisborne Chenin Blanc

If any dish will convert you to the wonderments of the underrated chenin blanc grape, this is it. In 1999, James made his chenin with a whisper of sweetness that is a perfect foil for the earthiness of puy lentils, and the subtle spiciness from its time in oak barrels ties in with the lemon thyme. The sharpness of the fennel accentuates the wine's fresh-fruit finish.

Millton wines are made from grapes grown biodynamically, according to the precepts of philosopher and educationalist, Rudolph Steiner. The company's chenin has a keen following, but the label is probably better known for a series of very stylish rieslings. Chardonnay, made in a couple of different guises, is another star in the line-up, and a merlot-dominant red blend is a popular buy at the cellar door. **VW**

Mills Reef Winery

The restaurant at Mills Reef Winery has a commanding position in the impressive winery building. This is a grand scale lunchtime restaurant and a very pleasant place to dine. Locals and tourists alike flock to enjoy the striking setting and fine food and wines. An elevated, curved terrace leads off from the dining room to conjoin the spectacular grounds, with views to the vines beyond.

A large tasting room adjacent to the restaurant accommodates many visitors and offers the chance to sample and buy the Mills Reef range of wines. Locals talk of memorable weekend 'pétanque and pizza' get-togethers. During any day, a trail of people can be seen walking the pathways that meander through the gardens, playing pétanque or simply enjoying the scenery and a glass of fine wine. **JLeC**

Chicken breasts in paper with orange pistachio stuffing & port wine sauce

SERVES 4

1 tblsp olive oil	1 tblsp chopped fresh chives
2 shallots, peeled and finely diced	1/4–1/2 cup orange juice
1 orange, skin, pith and seeds removed, flesh roughly chopped	sea salt and freshly ground black pepper
1/2 cup pistachio nuts, toasted and chopped	4 chicken breasts, trimmed
1 cup fresh breadcrumbs	4 lengths non-stick baking paper

1 Gently cook shallots in oil until softened. Mix shallots with remaining stuffing ingredients adding just enough orange juice to bind into a firm but not wet mixture, season with salt and pepper to taste.

2 Loosen skin from chicken breasts and pack stuffing between the skin and the breast. Place each chicken breast onto a large piece of baking paper, wrap tightly and lay in an oven dish. Bake for 20 minutes at 190°C.

3 Unwrap parcels to serve with port wine sauce.

PORT WINE SAUCE:

1 shallot, peeled and finely diced	1 cup beef stock
1 cup port	

1 Place shallot and port into a saucepan and bring to the boil. Simmer until reduced by half. Add beef stock; simmer to reduce to a sauce consistency. Season with salt to taste if necessary. Strain to serve.

Recipe created by chef Chris Pullin, Mills Reef Winery

Wine: Mills Reef Elspeth Syrah

The generous dollop of port in the sauce and orange juice in the stuffing makes this dish a challenge for any wine, but Paddy Preston's top-shelf syrah has the power and richness to handle it. Pistachio nuts are naturally tannic, but rather than increasing the perception of tannin in the wine, they soften it – a mysterious reaction that can be used to make a fierce young red more approachable.

Mills Reef earned a national reputation for red wines a couple of years ago when two of its products took two consecutive trophies at a major competition. Certainly, Paddy is a dab hand with the so-called Bordeaux varieties, cabernet sauvignon, merlot and cabernet franc, but he has also produced excellent riesling and gewürztraminer, as well as superbly ripe sauvignon blanc and a couple of big-fruited but stylish chardonnays. **VW**

Morton Estate

For many wine enthusiasts, Morton Estate Black Label Chardonnay was the wine that showed just how well this classic variety could do in the hands of a skilled winemaker. It has a lot more competition nowadays, but is still right up there with the best.

But there is much more to the Morton Estate story than this big-hearted white. The company produces a wide range of wines from grapes grown in Hawke's Bay and Marlborough. The black label also goes onto a seriously good blend of merlot and cabernet sauvignon, while several variations on the chardonnay and sauvignon blanc themes wear the less pricey white label. Sparkling wines are invariably excellent, and a pinot noir made from Marlborough grapes is one of the few bargains in its class. **vw**

Matawhero Wines

Mins Reef Winery

MATAWHERO WINES – THE OLD COLOSSEUM CAFÉ & WINE BAR

In the heart of the vineyards, the Colosseum Café and Wine Bar has been opened by the warm and wonderful owners of Matawhero Wines. Here you will find friendly hospitality and lively food cooked with generosity and talent. Wine and food pairing is part of the Irwins' passion, so it is not surprising that much enthusiasm goes into this aspect of their business. This spacious, attractive temple of food exhibits Italian links relating to Violet's ancestry; this Sicilian-inspired dish is to honour her lineage.

Also strangely reminiscent of Sicily, a powerful perfume of orange blossom hangs in the air surrounding this pretty piece of land. Later, walking through the pretty rambling garden at the Irwin homestead, layers of personality are revealed, and among the plantings a most beautiful rose. Internationally famous rose breeder Sam McGredy developed and named this rose 'Matawhero' because its heady perfume is his impression of a nicely aged gewürztraminer. **JLeC**

PORK CUTLETS WITH SICILIAN SAUCE

SERVES 4

1 each red, yellow and orange pepper
2 tblsp extra virgin olive oil
1 tblsp whole fennel seeds
2 tsp sugar
400g can tomato purée
8 small ripe tomatoes, quartered
4 pork cutlets, trimmed
sea salt and freshly ground black pepper

1 Remove core and seeds from all the peppers and slice flesh into thin strips. Heat oven to 180°C.
2 Heat a saucepan, add oil and fennel seeds and gently toast for 1 minute over a medium heat. Add sliced peppers and cook for 5–10 minutes to soften. Add sugar and tomato purée, bring to the boil and add quartered fresh tomatoes. Season with salt and pepper to taste.
3 Meanwhile, heat a large ovenproof frying pan, add a little oil and brown pork cutlets on both sides. Pour over hot tomato mixture and transfer to the oven for 10 minutes.

Recipe created by Julie Le Clerc

WINE: MATAWHERO RESERVE GEWÜRZTRAMINER

Gewürztraminer is often cited as the ideal wine for curry, but it is seldom a great match – it gained this reputation simply because it refuses to be intimidated by strong flavours. Pork, however, suits this super-aromatic variety very well indeed. Denis Irwin's Reserve bottling is usually dry, whereas the Estate version often carries a hint of sweetness. Either wine would sit well with this dish, but I believe the Reserve is the better choice because it has enough flavour intensity and fruit richness to match the strong flavours of the peppers and fennel seeds.

Matawhero Wines have been part of the New Zealand wine scene for many years. Denis refuses to follow established flavour trails, and is happy to hold bottles back from sale if he believes they will improve with age. It is an idiosyncratic approach that sometimes backfires, but when he gets it right his wines are among the best in the land. **VW**

HAWKE'S BAY

COULD EASILY LAY CLAIM TO BEING THE COUNTRY'S MOST VERSATILE WINE REGION.

Mission Estate

ITS REPUTATION HAS BEEN CARVED OUT with reds based on cabernet sauvignon and merlot, but it also produces elegant chardonnay, softly spoken sauvignon blanc, stylish riesling and excellent gewürztraminer.

And that is just the mainstream varieties. Syrah and viognier, both originally from France's Rhône Valley, also perform well in the Bay, and even zinfandel, the darling of California, shows promise.

It is appropriate that Hawke's Bay should play such an important part in the country's vinous jigsaw – it is, after all, where it all started. Mission Estate, founded in 1851, is the oldest winemaking concern still operated by its original owners, and across town Te Mata Estate still uses parts of the original winery buildings, erected in the 1870s.

The Bay's versatility can be attributed to the wide number of different soil types and climatic conditions within its boundaries. Vines have been planted everywhere, from the windswept coastal plains overlooking the Pacific to the foothills of the Ruahine and Kaweka Ranges. In between, stones littering the ground in the highly sought-after area known as Gimblett Gravels reflect the sun's rays and retain heat in the soil overnight, raising average temperatures by a useful few degrees. A few kilometres away, the soil is so fertile the vines grow masses of leaves that must be plucked off to allow the grapes to see the sun.

In these conditions, overcropping is a problem best tackled by the accountant-scaring policy of throwing away perfectly good ripening bunches to force extra flavour into those that remain.

Hawke's Bay is a booming centre for wine tourism, with several operators offering trips around the local wineries. Some of the smaller concerns are cautious about attracting crowds – the owner of one tiny property has been known to describe tourists as 'a bunch of tyre-kickers' – but most of the medium and larger companies are keen to show off their liquid wares and acquire a few extra names for their mailing lists.

And, of course, where there is good wine there is bound to be good food. The Bay offers a wide selection of restaurants, from tiny cafés to luxury lodges, and they are all proud to promote local produce.

That produce is presented direct to the public at regular farmers' markets, and many growers also run roadside stalls to attract passing trade from locals and visitors.

New Zealand wine is promoted overseas as 'the riches of a clean, green land', and nowhere does that slogan seem more appropriate than in lush, sunny Hawke's Bay. **VW**

Esk Valley Estate

Esk Valley Estate sits gently nestled among the hills of Bay View. Visitors are welcome to bring a picnic and sit in the gardens overlooking the sweeping vines and famous terraces and out towards a clear, blue sea. The sunny tasting rooms and umbrella-festooned balcony are also appealing places to linger and drink in the magic of Esk Valley wines.

This historic coastal winery has a quiet respect for tradition and makes fine handcrafted wines from selected vineyards. For example, the famous 'Terraces' is a single vineyard wine made from grapes grown on traditional terraced vines carved into the steep southern hillside of the estate. These vines enjoy all-day sun, producing well-rounded fruit, which tells this story later on from the bottle.

JLeC

Verjuice pickled prunes with blue cheese

MAKES 2 CUPS

1 cup hot tea (I like to use aromatic Earl Grey)

250g pitted prunes

1 cup cabernet sauvignon Verjuice

1/4 cup sugar

juice and pared rind of 1 lemon

1 cinnamon stick

8 whole cloves

8 whole black peppercorns

2 blades mace (a culinary spice – optional if hard to procure)

1. Pour hot tea over prunes and leave to soak overnight.
2. Next day, mix remaining ingredients together in a saucepan and boil for 5 minutes.
3. Add prunes and tea and simmer for a further 5 minutes. Stand to cool and allow flavours to infuse.
4. Serve alongside New Zealand Kikorangi or similar creamy blue cheese and crackers.

Recipe created by Julie Le Clerc

Wine: Esk Valley Reserve Merlot/Malbec/Cabernet Sauvignon

Gordon Russell's massive but stylish three-grape blend is sometimes referred to as a little brother to The Terraces, but that doesn't give it enough credit – it is a seriously good wine in its own right. Gordon chose the 1998 vintage to accompany Julie's prune and cheese platter, but later vintages should do the job just as well. This is an example of selecting a wine to go with the accessories on the plate. Blue cheese is often partnered by a sweet dessert wine, but in this case it is the prunes that go particularly well with the berry characters in the cabernet component, and soften the rustic earthiness of the malbec.

Esk Valley's reds enjoy a big following, but the label is also worn by an approachable sauvignon blanc, a nicely balanced riesling, and a chardonnay that has won several awards through various vintages. Gordon is one of a handful of winemakers in the country to take chenin blanc seriously. His chunky but stylish reading of the style is well worth searching out.

VW

Church Road Winery

Outdoor tables and chairs under a cluster of large leafy trees make Church Road winery a very pleasant place to pause. Barbecues are held outdoors in the summer months and lunch is also served in the indoor dining area. Some great compositions come out of the professional kitchen, and a nice touch to the menu is a 'food and wine match of the week' suggestion.

Church Road winery also features a wine shop, a function room, and a winemaking museum (the only one of its kind in New Zealand), which traces a fascinating journey through the history and techniques of winemaking in this country.

This pretty dessert can be served with poached tamarillos when in season, or any other fruit such as luscious fresh peaches or berries. **JLeC**

Honey & cinnamon wafers with vanilla mascarpone cream

SERVES 4

50g butter

2 tblsp liquid honey (use a honey with good flavour)

5 sheets filo pastry

1 tblsp cinnamon to dust

1 Pre-heat oven to 175°C. Melt butter and honey together and use to brush onto sheets of filo pastry, layering each sheet on top of the previous sheet. Use a 6cm pastry cutter to cut out 16 circles and place onto a baking sheet lined with non-stick baking paper.

2 Dust with cinnamon and bake for 5–8 minutes until golden and crisp. Remove to cool.

VANILLA MASCARPONE CREAM:

1/2 cup mascarpone (a type of strained thickened cream)

1/2 cup cream

1 tblsp icing sugar

1 vanilla bean

1 Place mascarpone, cream and icing sugar into a bowl. Cut vanilla bean in half lengthways and scrape out seeds with a fine tipped knife. Add vanilla seeds to cream mixture and whip to soft peaks.

2 Layer 4 wafers per person with spoonfuls of vanilla mascarpone cream. Serve with seasonal fruit.

Recipe created by chef Jeremy Trotter, Church Road

Wine: Montana Virtu Noble Sémillon

Honey, cinnamon, vanilla – this dish pushes all the dessert wine flavour buttons. The 'Noble' in the name tells us the grapes were infected by the so-called 'noble rot', botrytis. Decidedly undesirable when the grapes are destined for dry wine, this unsightly looking substance is treasured when sweetness is the aim. Rain can turn it into unwanted wet rot within hours, but when the days and nights stay dry, botrytis insinuates itself over the surface of the grapes, sending probing fingers through the pores in the skin to suck out all the water content. Left sitting on the vine, the grapes end up looking like mouldy raisins – but they produce the most luscious beverages in the winemaker's portfolio.

The Church Road winery is industry giant Montana's shop window in the Bay. Church Road Chardonnay is one of the country's most popular restaurant wines, and the reds in the range, made with input from the French house of Cordier, are consistently excellent. **VW**

Craig Farm Winery

Church Road Winery

Mission Estate

Esk Valley Estate

CRAB FARM WINERY

The thought that this is a strange name for a winery must run through every visitor's mind when arriving at Crab Farm. Originally the land was covered in tidal water, reeds and crabs, but the great Hawke's Bay earthquake of 1931 lifted the land at Crab Farm above sea level, creating the site of the present-day vineyard and winery.

The Vineyard Restaurant is a casual eatery providing pleasant food well suited to Crab Farm's superb food-friendly wines. The distinctive and rustic courtyard dining area is a pleasant place to sit and relax in vine-leaf dappled sunlight. Here, every possible use has cleverly been found for old wine barrels, from whimsical water features to planters, tables and surprisingly comfortable armchairs.

JLeC

GURNARD FILLETS WITH LEMON CAPER SAUCE

SERVES 4

1 cup fish stock
finely grated zest and juice of 1 lemon
1 tsp brown sugar
good pinch saffron tips (Black Pearl is a good brand)
1/4 cup cream
1/4 cup salted capers, rinsed and drained
sea salt and freshly ground black pepper
4 gurnard fillets, bones removed and cleaned
lemon wedges to serve

1 Bring fish stock to the boil and then simmer to reduce by half. Add lemon zest and juice, brown sugar and saffron, stirring until sugar dissolves. Stir in cream and capers. Season with salt and pepper to taste.
2 Heat a pan or grill and cook fish fillets, turning once.
3 Spoon sauce over fish and serve immediately with lemon wedges on the side.

Recipe created by chef Kees Peters, Crab Farm Vineyard Restaurant

WINE: CRAB FARM CHARDONNAY

This dish is tailor-made for chardonnay. On its own, this classic variety is quite citric, but it is a grape that adapts well to winery techniques, and each step in its production adds extra aromas and flavours. Here, the lemon rind ties in with the wine's basic character, and the cream matches the creamy texture the wine has acquired through being allowed to undergo a malolactic fermentation, a natural process that converts sharp malic acids to softer lactic acids. The saffron and capers provide accents that echo the spicy oak. Hamish Jardine chose a 1997 vintage to go with the dish, because he felt the softness acquired during its maturation made it a better match.

Crab Farm has a keen following for both red and white wines, few of which bother to follow vinous fashion. A world-class merlot and a well-focused cabernet sauvignon share shelf space with a couple of nicely structured sweet wines, and the cellar shop can usually offer two or three chardonnays of different styles and vintages. **VW**

Duck liver salad with prosciutto, roasted tomatoes & balsamic dressing

SERVES 4

8 medium tomatoes, halved

sea salt and freshly ground black pepper

extra virgin olive oil

12 thin slices prosciutto

1/4 cup flour

12 duck livers, trimmed

1/4 cup quality balsamic vinegar

1 tsp brown sugar

2 tblsp olive oil

2 cups mesclun (mixed baby salad leaves)

1/2 cup Parmesan shavings

1 Pre-heat oven to 120°C. Lay tomato halves onto an oven tray cut side up. Season with salt and pepper and drizzle with olive oil. Slow roast in oven for 3 hours until semi-dried.

2 Lay prosciutto onto a lightly oiled oven tray and roast for 5 minutes until crisp.

3 Season flour with salt and pepper. Heat a pan with a little olive oil. Dust duck livers with seasoned flour and sear in pan. Place into oven to finish cooking at 180°C for 3–4 minutes until firm to touch but still pink inside.

4 Add balsamic vinegar to release flavoursome residue from pan. Add brown sugar, 2 tblsp olive oil and season with salt and pepper to form a dressing.

5 To assemble, layer all ingredients onto serving plates. Drizzle with juices from the pan.

Recipe created by chef Steve Beere, Mission Restaurant

Wine: Mission Estate Reserve Pinot Gris

In Europe it is assumed that as long as all the components in the glass and on the plate are local, they will complement one another. The classic partner for duck livers is a sweet white, but this alternative pairing takes the original home of the grape into account. Pinot gris comes from Alsace, where goose and duck products feature in a large number of dishes. The Mission Reserve interpretation of the style is dry, but boasts enough fruit depth to stand up to the richness of the livers. Its other qualities pick up on the secondary flavours in the dish – it is a chunky wine, which ties in with the outspoken characters of the prosciutto, and its grainy edge matches the Parmesan. Finally, the grape's natural sweetness is accentuated by the sauce.

Mission Estate produces a wide range of red and white wines, invariably sharply priced. Top of the tree are the Reserve and Jewelstone labels, but awards have been received right through the range. **VW**

Mission Estate

It's a grand drive from the entrance gates, winery and vineyard of 150-year-old Mission Estate up to the distinctive original building on the hill. Divine views extend from the former seminary building, a richly historic place established by French Catholic missionaries. Early vintages were produced purely for sacramental purposes, of course, but as demand for the Brothers' wine increased so did the sales.

The original building now houses the Mission restaurant, where major alterations are underway to modernise the space. In the kitchen, the chef's philosophy is to 'cook the classics with a modern influence', and innovation is achieved with a gentle approach and brilliant results. Whenever possible, organic main ingredients are sourced from local suppliers, and the kitchen enjoys working with the freshest Hawke's Bay ingredients. **JLeC**

Sacred Hill Wines

Sacred Hill's name is derived from the translation of Puketapu, the small village near the Mason family home in the Dartmoor Valley. The winery is tucked into a unique native bush setting where picnic tables are scattered under trees, and fabulous food and their seriously stylish wines are served over the summer months.

The philosophy of Sacred Hill is 'all about involving people' and this is evident in every aspect of the property. There is an edge of excitement here, a sense of style, dedication and an affirmation that it is possible to live and breathe wine.

Wine, food and people are regularly combined at Sacred Hill and one of the exclusively divine experiences to be captured is 'Dining with Angels'. This event may take the form of a progressive dinner around the vineyards, or an unforgettable evening of elegant dining ensconced in a pretty candlelit dell. In true Sacred Hill style, fond memories of good company, a series of delicious dishes and stunning wines are assured. **JLeC**

Slow-baked salmon with saffron & verjuice beurre blanc

SERVES 4

BEURRE BLANC:

1 tblsp finely chopped shallots

1 1/2 tblsp fresh lemon or lime juice

4 tblsp Riesling Verjuice

1/2 cup cream

175g butter, cubed

pinch or two of saffron powder

sea salt

1 Combine shallots, lemon or lime juice and verjuice in a pan and reduce rapidly until nearly evaporated. Add cream and reduce over medium heat until slightly thickened.

2 Transfer to a double boiler so that sauce is gently heated; be careful not to let it boil. Whisk in butter, a few cubes at a time, until just melted and sauce is thick. Add saffron and season with salt to taste.

SALMON:

600–700g fresh salmon fillet, skin on, fine pin bones removed

sea salt and freshly ground black pepper

1 Cut salmon into four portions. Heat a pan until very hot, add a little olive oil and seal salmon pieces until just beginning to brown.

2 Season with salt and pepper and place in an oven pan. Transfer to an oven pre-heated to 140°C and cook for 15–18 minutes (depending on thickness) until heated through and medium rare.

3 To serve, neatly arrange salmon on top of, for example, sliced baked potato. Spoon sauce over salmon and serve immediately with a green vegetable such as spinach.

Recipe created by chef Mike Williams, Sacred Hill Winery

Wine: Sacred Hill Rifleman's Reserve Chardonnay

Cooking salmon rare or medium-rare increases its flavour intensity, and makes it an excellent companion for this big fruited, oak-edged chardonnay. They're serious food lovers at Sacred Hill, and their wines are designed to be enjoyed as part of a meal, not analysed in isolation. That fits right into the ethos of this book. The Sacred Hill star is definitely on the ascendant. The portfolio varies from year to year, but it usually includes a couple of variations on the chardonnay theme, and a handful of thoughtfully made reds. Both styles have won top awards. Idiosyncratic but highly successful extras include a sauvignon blanc sub-labelled 'sauvage' to reflect the fact that it is fermented with wild yeasts rather than 'tame' laboratory-bred versions, and an occasional dessert wine. **VW**

Te Awa Farm Winery

Te Awa o te Atua, the full place name in Maori, means River of God, a reference to the mysterious subterranean streams over which Te Awa Farm is situated and from which its wines draw their subliminal character.

Producing quality wines that are 'made to be enjoyed with food' led to the establishment of this stylish restaurant to provide a unique dining experience. With enthusiasm and commitment wines are paired with intensely creative cooking based principally around local produce. Te Awa Farm also owns two properties dedicated to growing certified organic vegetables to provide the ingredients on which the restaurant dishes are based. At Te Awa Farm the wine, the food and the farm-fresh produce combine to reveal a memorable experience that is more than the sum of its parts. Taste this experience à la carte, indoors or outside in the beautiful grounds complete with large pétanque terrain. **JLeC**

Potato soufflés with crayfish, asparagus & smoked paprika oil

SERVES 4

SMOKED PAPRIKA OIL:

1 onion, finely chopped

1/2 cup extra virgin olive oil

1 tblsp La Chinata Spanish smoked sweet paprika

1 Gently cook onion in 2 tblsp of the oil until softened without colouring. Add smoked paprika and remaining olive oil. Bring to the boil then immediately remove from the heat to a bowl. Leave to infuse for 3 hours. Strain through a fine sieve. Reserve infused oil.

POTATO SOUFFLÉS:

1 cup cooked potato purée

3 tblsp grated fresh Parmesan cheese

2 egg yolks

1 tblsp cream

sea salt and freshly ground black pepper

3 egg whites

2–3 crayfish tails, delicately cooked and sliced

fresh asparagus tips, blanched

coriander to garnish

1 Mix potato purée, Parmesan, yolks and cream together. Season with salt and pepper.
2 Whisk egg whites to soft peaks and gently fold into first mixture.
3 Place mixture into 4 greased ramekins, cover loosely with foil and steam in a water bath for 10 minutes until risen.
4 Turn out soufflés onto serving plates. Decorate with sliced crayfish and fresh asparagus when in season. Drizzle with smoked paprika oil and garnish with coriander.

Recipe created and styled by chef Rick Rutledge-Manning, Te Awa Farm Winery

Wine: Te Awa Farm Longlands Chardonnay

This wine match pays due respect to the major ingredient on the plate, but it also takes heed of the dish's minor players. Crayfish has a natural sweetness that suits the core flavours of ripe-fruited chardonnay, but the processes used in Longlands' creation have been taken into account. The barrels in which it matures are charred on the inside, and this is echoed by the smoky character of the paprika. The grainy notes of good Parmesan reflect the mealiness picked up when the wine is 'lees-stirred', a technique that involves stirring the spent yeast into the wine to give it extra flavour. Finally, the cream matches the texture added through a partial malolactic fermentation.

Te Awa Farm's Jenny Dobson honed her winemaking skills during a stint at Château Senejac, in Bordeaux, France, and her style reflects this European experience. Her merlot and cabernet-based reds are world-beaters, and her syrah is poised to follow in their footsteps. **VW**

SILENI ESTATES

Sileni is an imposing statement on the vinous landscape. Sweeping up the driveway to be greeted by manicured gardens and a grand entranceway makes a bold impression. They are serious about food and wine at Sileni, and aim to showcase the best of Hawke's Bay produce.

The estates' Epicurean Centre and Cellar was developed to give visitors a total wine and food destination experience. Here, it is possible to take cooking classes and wine education classes, participate in wine tastings, shop in the food store for hard-to-find ingredients, or dine elegantly or casually in one of the two distinctly different eating spaces.

Both Sileni restaurants have adjunct culinary gardens planted with pretty quince and fig trees and every type of herb imaginable. Great thought is taken in the use of these herbs in the kitchen. A bonus is that the plants release their delicious and aromatic essential oils to fill the warm air wafting over the outside dining area. **JLeC**

Sileni Estates' head, Graeme Avery, is passionate about promoting the wine and produce of Hawke's Bay to the rest of New Zealand and the world. Sileni wines made quite a splash in their first vintage, winning several rave reviews here and overseas. Frost damage decimated the home vineyards prior to the 2001 vintage, but winemaker Grant Edmonds performed his magic with contract-grown grapes to keep the name right up there with the best.

Top of the Sileni heap is a merlot-based blend called EV. The initials stand for 'Exceptional Vintage', and the wine will be produced only when conditions allow. A couple of other merlot-dominant reds, a full-flavoured chardonnay and a hugely flavoursome sémillon are among highlights of the portfolio. Dining at either of the Sileni restaurants, RD-1 or the more casual Mesa, while enjoying Sileni wines by the glass is invariably a memorable experience. **VW**

Sacred Hill Wines

Pepper-cured beef with mint & walnut pesto

SERVES 4

MINT AND WALNUT PESTO:

1 clove garlic, peeled

1/2 cup fresh mint leaves

1/4 cup fresh walnuts, lightly toasted

1/4 cup grated Parmesan

1/4 cup walnut oil (try KerNelZ New
   Zealand grown and pressed for freshness)
   or extra virgin olive oil

sea salt to taste

1 Blend all ingredients to form a smooth paste.

PEPPER-CURED BEEF:

500g premium beef tenderloin eye
   fillet, trimmed

5 tblsp freshly crushed black peppercorns

3/4 cup raw sugar

1 cup rock salt

3 tblsp cognac

1 Roll beef in cracked peppercorns to evenly cover.
2 Mix sugar, salt and cognac together and pack onto beef to fully encase meat. Cover tightly with plastic wrap and refrigerate for 2 days, turning every 12 hours.
3 After 2 days remove beef from resulting liquid and dry well on paper towels. Slice thinly, lay on top of, for example, roasted eggplant and pickling onions tossed in paprika, toasted walnuts and olives. Top with mint and walnut pesto to serve.

Recipe created by Julie Le Clerc

Wine: Stonecroft Syrah

'You've got to try Stonecroft.' That's the advice any visiting wine buff will be given if he or she asks about New Zealand syrah. Alan and Glen Limmer's most famous red is made in tiny quantities, but it has an international reputation. We can thank the couple's stubbornness for its existence – the experts told them the variety wouldn't ripen properly in New Zealand's relatively cool climate.

This dish has several points of contact with the wine. The richness of the beef is the major link, but the coating of cracked pepper ties in with one of the classic characters of ripe syrah. Eggplant's natural smokiness, enhanced by roasting, picks up the suggestion of charred oak, and the tannins in the walnuts pull alongside the tannins in the wine, mysteriously softening one another to enrich the mouthfeel.

It is syrah that has made the Stonecroft label famous, but the Limmers also produce a startlingly good gewürztraminer that they love to partner with Indonesian food. A chunky chardonnay, an approachable sauvignon blanc and an exceedingly rare zinfandel are also part of their small portfolio. **VW**

Stonecroft

Stonecroft is a family owned and operated boutique winery. Here, personality pervades both the place and the charismatic wines. From Stonecroft's enthusiastic and generous owners to the hand-labelled bottles (the sketched logo was drawn by a friend), to the bounding welcome from Tommy and Chloe, the vineyard's good-natured boxer dogs, a feeling of warmth and great integrity prevails.

Maximum effort was put into selecting the vineyard sites and their development has been aimed at producing high quality fruit. All harvesting is by hand and the winemaking is traditional, following a founding mission statement 'to produce full-bodied, elegant, fruit-driven wines'. A landmark for Stonecroft was the inaugural release of Syrah in 1989, New Zealand's first commercial release of this variety in recent times. This is a heady wine with a dense wild berry fruit nose, intense Syrah mid-palate and a lingering pepper-spice finish. **JLeC**

Ngatarawa Wines

Ngatarawa Wines is a most graceful and elegant property. The winery and cellar door are housed in huge converted stables that 100 years ago accommodated racehorses, hence one of the wine labels, 'The Stables'. A beautiful water lily garden sits in a large pond surrounded by clipped green grass; the vines spread far off into the distance. Relaxing on the lawn seating with the gentle sound of water trickling from the fountain has a dreamy, somnolent effect.

Alwyn Corban pioneered grape growing and winemaking in the Ngatarawa district and is himself a fourth generation winemaker. Ngatarawa wines are beautifully crafted; here is the stuff that dreams are made of.

Note: Verjuice is the unfermented juice of unripe grapes and is used to make this unusual and deliciously refreshing dessert. Try it with the straw-gold coloured Stables Late Harvest Riesling, served lightly chilled – it's ideal with the jelly, fresh fruit and lashings of cream. **JLeC**

Hawke's Bay cabernet sauvignon verjuice jelly with raspberries

SERVES 6

SUGAR SYRUP:

1/2 cup sugar

1/2 cup water

1 Mix sugar and water together in a small saucepan. Slowly bring to the boil stirring until sugar dissolves. Boil for one minute then remove to cool. Sugar syrup can be stored indefinitely in the refrigerator.

VERJUICE JELLY:

4 leaves gelatine (or substitute 3 tsp powdered gelatine)

2 cups Cabernet Sauvignon Verjuice

1/2 cup sugar syrup (above)

1 Cover gelatine leaves with cold water and leave to soften.
2 Bring verjuice and sugar syrup to the boil. Squeeze gelatine to remove excess water then add and whisk until dissolved.
3 Pour into serving cups or glasses and allow to set in refrigerator for 3–4 hours. Top with fresh raspberries and serve with whipped cream.

Recipe created by Julie Le Clerc

Wine: Stables Late Harvest Riesling

And now for something completely different! Since the verjuice is made from cabernet sauvignon, it might be supposed that a red wine would be the logical accompaniment. In fact, the major flavours in the dish are quite citric, even though no lemons or limes are used. The jelly is not intensely sweet, and that makes it a good match for this gentle and stylish wine.

Alwyn Corban is a serious and dedicated winemaker who has achieved good medal success. The label is most commonly associated with reds based on cabernet sauvignon and merlot, but a number of excellent wines have been made from chardonnay and sauvignon blanc grapes over the years, as well as several stand-out dessert styles. Wines wearing the Glazebrook and Alwyn labels are top of the tree, while the Stables range is pitched lower in the market. At all levels, they are invariably well-made and offer excellent value. **VW**

Prosciutto & tarragon-wrapped fillet steak

SERVES 4

600–800g premium beef tenderloin eye fillet, trimmed

2 cloves garlic, chopped

3 tblsp extra virgin olive oil

1/2 cup CJ Pask Merlot

3 tblsp freshly chopped tarragon

12 thin slices prosciutto

8 small beetroot, cooked, peeled and quartered

1/4–1/2 cup shaved fresh Parmesan

1 Cut beef into four steaks and place into a non-reactive bowl with garlic, oil and wine. Leave to marinate for one hour.

2 Drain steaks and discard liquid. Rub steaks with chopped tarragon and wrap in prosciutto so that they become parcels.

3 Heat grill or frying pan and cook steak parcels for about 3 minutes on each side for rare, depending on thickness of meat and preference for pinkness.

4 Serve with beetroot and shavings of fresh Parmesan.

Recipe created by Julie Le Clerc

Wine: CJ Pask Reserve Merlot

Beetroot is the secret ingredient in this wine and food match – its sharp but faintly sweet flavours are a perfect foil to merlot's natural richness. The beef is a natural partner, and the smoky, faintly salty notes of prosciutto and Parmesan enhance the link.

Merlot is an approachable grape that was originally planted to fill what was perceived as a 'flavour hole' in the middle of local wines made solely from cabernet sauvignon, but in recent years it has become a star in its own right. Kate Radburnd has made some excellent wines from it, sometimes blending it but often leaving it to fly solo. Chris Pask pioneered the region now known as Gimblett Gravels, and his company enjoys a solid reputation right through its range. The emphasis is on reds, but chardonnay and a stylish sparkling wine are both worth searching out. **VW**

CJ Pask Winery

Dry riverbed shingle-based free-draining soil is a feature of Gimblett Road vineyards. The river stones retain heat, increase soil temperature and reflect sun onto the grapes during the day and then release warmth long after the sun has set. This natural heating system effectively extends the grape-ripening process and heightens the fruit characteristics in the resulting wine. Elegant CJ Pask wines are crafted and cared for on-site to ensure all the opportunities of Gimblett Road are reflected in the final product.

This is a great place to visit during the region's annual Harvest Hawke's Bay weekend celebration. An impressive way to feed crowds of visitors was demonstrated with exotic burgers flame-grilled on a barbecue and devoured with accompanying CJ Pask wines and live music in the barrel room. **JLeC**

VIDAL ESTATE

Vidal Estate is an original and historic winery in Hawke's Bay. It seems unusual to find a winery in the centre of town, but the city of Hastings grew up and around the existing buildings. However, Vidal's continues to operate very nicely from its urban position through its dynamic tasting and sales cellar, wine bar, restaurant and appealing alfresco dining area.

This recipe for a deliciously different salad employs a hot-smoking method to cook the lamb. This is not difficult and definitely worth attempting, although barbecuing would serve the purpose at a pinch.

Note: To hot-smoke, form an open container from a piece of foil and fill with two handfuls of tea leaves or fine wood shavings. Place this in the bottom of a dry wok or large frying pan. Place a rack elevated over the smoking mix. Put lamb onto the rack. Cover entire pan with foil and/or a tight lid to prevent smoke escaping. Place pan over medium heat for 10–15 minutes. Remove from heat and open gently to remove lamb. Dispose of smoking mix carefully. **JLeC**

SMOKED LAMB, FENNEL, BASIL, FIG & MOZZARELLA SALAD WITH VERJUICE DRESSING

SERVES 4

2 lamb hearts of rump, seared in a hot pan
small bunch fresh basil leaves
12 dried mission figs
1 bulb fresh fennel, trimmed and very finely sliced
150g fresh mozzarella, thickly sliced
2 cups mesclun (mixed baby lettuce leaves)

VERJUICE DRESSING:

1/4 cup Hawke's Bay Riesling Verjuice
1/4 cup extra virgin olive oil
finely grated zest of 1 lemon
1/4 cup roughly chopped summer herbs, including fennel
sea salt and freshly ground black pepper

1 Hot-smoke seared lamb rumps (see note opposite) or alternatively, barbecue lamb to give a smoky flavour.
2 Allow meat to rest for 10 minutes before slicing thinly.
3 To deep fry basil, dry basil leaves well and carefully deep fry very briefly in hot oil. Drain well on paper towels. Reserve to garnish salad.
4 Whisk vinaigrette ingredients together and season with salt and pepper to taste.
5 Toss all salad ingredients together in dressing and serve.

Recipe created by chef Kylie Howard, Vidal Estate

WINE: VIDAL HAWKE'S BAY RESERVE CHARDONNAY

This wine has done well for the Vidal team in its last few vintages. It has picked up a few awards, including, in 1998 colours, the Top Chardonnay trophy at the New Zealand Wine Society Royal Easter Wine Show. Red wine is the traditional accompaniment to lamb, but there are so many other flavours happening in this dish that a bit of lateral thinking was necessary. The wine has a smoky edge that suits the cooking treatment, but the major links are from the plate's 'extras' – fennel, figs and basil are all great partners for barrel-aged chardonnay.

Vidal is part of the Villa Maria group, but it is run as a separate operation. Only the best wines wear the Reserve label, but the less exalted Estate collection contains a few well-priced gems in most vintages. The company enjoys a good reputation through its entire range, with chardonnay heading the white list and blends based on cabernet sauvignon and merlot the best-known reds. **VW**

ROASTED PUMPKIN & BLUE CHEESE PIES

SERVES 6

400g savoury short crust pastry

3 cups cubed pumpkin

2 tblsp olive oil

4 leeks, whites only

4 cloves garlic, finely chopped

2cm piece fresh ginger, finely chopped

1 1/2 tsp each ground cumin and coriander

1 1/2 tsp each curry powder and garam marsala

300g blue cheese, crumbled

sea salt and freshly ground black pepper

1 egg yolk

2 tblsp black or white sesame seeds

thick yoghurt to serve

1　Roll out pastry to 3mm thick and use to line 6 giant muffin tins. Chill well.

2　Rub pumpkin with olive oil and place into an oven pan. Roast at 200°C for 30 minutes until soft.

3　Thinly slice leeks and cook with a little oil in a pan until soft and translucent. Add garlic, ginger and spices. Cook for 2 minutes to release fragrance.

4　Combine pumpkin and leek mixture and set aside to cool. Once cold add crumbled blue cheese and season with salt and pepper to taste.

5　Spoon cold filling into chilled pastry cases. Roll out remaining pastry and cut out 6 circles to fit as lids to pies. Brush with egg yolk to seal and glaze. Sprinkle with sesame seeds and pierce pastry lids to release steam.

6　Bake at 200°C for 20 minutes until golden brown. Serve with thick yoghurt.

Recipe created by chef Jenny Parton, Brookfields Vineyards

WINE: BROOKFIELDS PINOT GRIS

Along with Mission Vineyards, Brookfields pioneered pinot gris in Hawke's Bay. Peter Robertson's style usually has faintly pear-like aromas, and a good quota of richly ripe fruit. The grape's natural sweetness picks up the same character in the pumpkin and blue cheese, and its distinctive graininess ties in with the Asian spices.

Brookfields is a well-respected company with a solid portfolio of whites and reds. Top of the heap is the brilliant gold label Reserve Cabernet Sauvignon/Merlot, but very good wines are also made from riesling, gewürztraminer and chardonnay. **VW**

BROOKFIELDS VINEYARDS

Brookfields is an engaging location, an oasis set amid the vines. The setting alone offers much satisfaction, with a rose garden pathway leading to the terrace and expansive outdoor seating area. Artwork adorns the interesting barrel room where functions are often held. Brookfields provides a warm welcome, skilful restaurant fare, attentive service and often a little jazz or classical music – moments that are all part of the Brookfields culture.

The restaurant offers a meticulous and consistent dining experience of carefully thought out and well-executed dishes with international flavours. Brookfields wines are fruit driven, which means they age well, rewarding those who resist temptation and cellar them. Diners are encouraged to pair wine and food for the enhancement of both.

JLeC

Brookfields Vineyards

CABERNET SAUVIGNON

Announcing the TRINITY HILL WINE COUNTRY CELLAR.

Savour the anticipation of receiving — or giving — a GIFT Box containing 2 selected, fine

TRINITY HILL

Trinity Hill Winery is surrounded by the most alluring sculptured gardens. Much thought, care and attention has been put into this space; imagine the attention to detail that goes into the winemaking! What a pleasure it is to pass through the calm, attractive, friendly winery and out into a hidden garden full of delightful 'rooms', surprising stone sculptures and pretty picnic spots. There is no restaurant on-site but simple hampers filled with foods orientated towards each wine style are planned to enhance the wine and food experience at Trinity Hill.

As guardians of the vines, the viticulturist and winemaker take what they describe as a 'minimalist' approach, coaxing, encouraging and managing what they feel is a very natural process. Trinity Hill winemakers combine modern equipment with traditional techniques to achieve their aim of making 'distinctly individual wines of elegance and power that reflect the character of the land'. **JLeC**

TURKEY, CORN & RED ONION SALAD WITH SEED MUSTARD DRESSING

SERVES 4

750g double turkey breast
2 ears sweetcorn
1 red onion, peeled and very finely diced
1/2 cup quality sundried tomatoes, halved
1/4 cup fresh basil leaves

DRESSING:

2 tblsp whole grain mustard
3 tblsp sherry vinegar (I particularly enjoy the flavour
 of Romulo sherry vinegar from Jerez in Spain)
1/4–1/2 cup extra virgin olive oil
sea salt and freshly ground black pepper

1   Pre-heat oven to 190°C. Cut turkey breast into 2 single breast portions, place in an oven pan, drizzle with olive oil, season with salt and pepper and roast for 25–30 minutes or until juices run clear. Remove to cool. Once cold, slice thinly.
2   Steam sweetcorn for 3 minutes, allow to cool. Once cold remove kernels with a sharp knife.
3   Place turkey slices, corn kernels, diced red onion and sundried tomatoes into a large bowl.
4   Blend dressing ingredients together, seasoning with salt and pepper to taste. Pour over salad ingredients and toss well. Serve scattered with basil leaves.

Recipe created by Julie Le Clerc

WINE: TRINITY HILL GIMBLETT ROAD CHARDONNAY

This is a match of textures as much as flavours. Warren Gibson's top-shelf chardonnay is superbly smooth as a result of careful oak ageing and a partial malolactic fermentation, and that makes it a great partner for the equally smooth turkey breast. It is a multi-layered wine, and most of its flavour notes find something to pair up with in the salad. The corn works well with the oak spice, and the onions pick up on the well-tuned acids.

Under the astute management of local winemaking icon, John Hancock, Trinity Hill has made a big splash in quite a short time. The Gimblett Road designation is reserved for the top labels, but there is quality right through the range. Gutsy but stylish chardonnays and powerful but elegant reds based on cabernet sauvignon and merlot are the stars, and a slightly rarer syrah looks exceedingly promising. **VW**

CLEARVIEW ESTATE WINERY

Clearview Estate Winery not only produces top quality wines but also operates a popular, well-established restaurant from its unique coastal location. This seaside setting gives a distinctly Mediterranean feel to the place. The sea breezes help to moderate temperature variance over the vines during their growing season, producing intense, vibrant and definitely not subtle wines, just as the winemaker desires them to be.

Select a table in the courtyard among grapevines, avocado trees, herbs and spreading old olive trees in summer, or inside by the log fire in winter. Local seasonal produce, olives, avocados and herbs from the winery gardens feature and the cooking style reflects the location. Choose a great wine and pair it with something tasty to eat from the à la carte menu, sit back and partake. **JLeC**

FRIED RED WINE BREAD

SERVES 8

1 1/2 cups warm water
1 tblsp sugar
1 tblsp active dry yeast
750g high grade flour
1 tblsp salt
1/2 cup pumpkin seeds
1/2 cup raisins
1/4 cup extra virgin olive oil
2 cups Clearview Estate red wine
extra olive oil for frying

1 Mix 1/2 cup of measured warm water with sugar and yeast. Leave in a warm place for 5 minutes to activate.

2 Place flour, salt, pumpkin seeds and raisins into the bowl of a mixer. Add oil and activated yeast mixture and 1 cup measured warm water. Mix together, adding more flour or water if necessary to bring to a firm dough consistency.

3 Knead with a dough hook or by hand for 5–10 minutes. Place in an oiled bowl covered with plastic wrap until doubled in size.

4 Knock back dough by pressing firmly with fist. Knead for 5 minutes. Shape into 2 rounds or place into oiled loaf tins. Leave to rise until doubled in size for 30–60 minutes.

5 Bake in an oven preheated to 175°C for 25–30 minutes. Remove to cool.

6 Cut 8 thick slices of the bread (best when day-old). Dip briefly into a shallow tray filled with red wine. Heat a pan, add a generous amount of olive oil and fry bread over high heat turning once until golden brown on both sides. Serve with avocado.

Recipe created by chef Stuart McGechan and baker Matthew Mills, Clearview Estate

WINE: CLEARVIEW OLD OLIVE BLOCK RESERVE

The blend varies from year to year, but cabernet franc, merlot and cabernet sauvignon are usually involved. This big, solid wine invariably has loads of rich fruit balanced by nicely focused oak. It works well with the bread, particularly if it is the red wine you choose for dipping, but as an alternative, Clearview Chardonnay would tie in nicely with the avocado.

Clearview wines are sold mainly at the cellar door and by mail order, but a few cases make it out to the general retail trade each year. There's no doubt this rarity enhances their reputation, but it would be justified even if more was made. Concentrated flavour is their key character right through the range. Tim Turvey doesn't make wine for wimps! **VW**

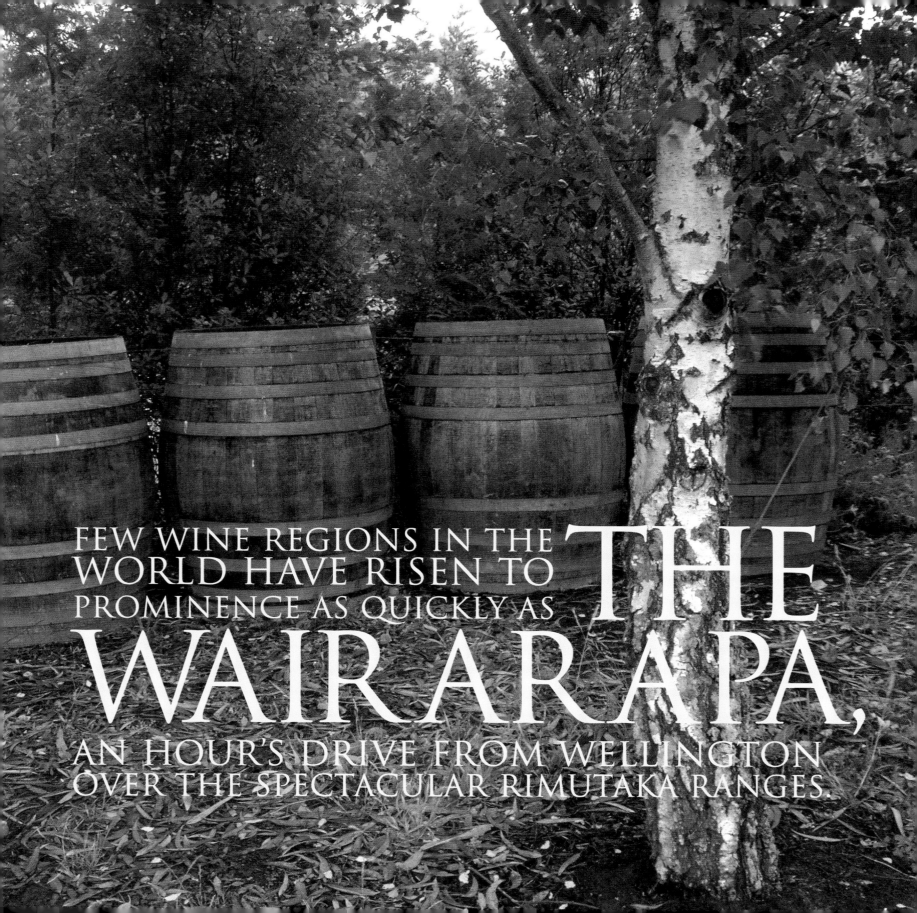

FEW WINE REGIONS IN THE WORLD HAVE RISEN TO PROMINENCE AS QUICKLY AS THE WAIRARAPA, AN HOUR'S DRIVE FROM WELLINGTON OVER THE SPECTACULAR RIMUTAKA RANGES.

THE LOCAL INDUSTRY IS CENTRED on Martinborough, a tiny rural township that few winelovers had heard of until the mid-1980s. The first labels to trickle onto the shelves were from Chifney Wines, Martinborough Vineyards, Ata Rangi and Dry River, all situated within a few minutes of the town centre.

There is a reason for their geographic proximity. The region's most sought-after vineyard sites are on the terrace that sits above the surrounding farmland, ensuring good drainage on even the wettest days. Properties on this higher ground command a price premium, although many other excellent sites have been identified and planted as the Wairarapa boom has continued. Viticulturists look for dry, gravelly soil, and they have found it scattered right throughout the province.

Pinot noir is king in the Wairarapa. Notorious for its fussiness, this classic variety presents a challenge to every grape grower and winemaker. Get it right, and it makes the most seductive red wine in the world. But even minor glitches in the weather can dilute the flavour and harden the flavour profile.

The Wairarapa is perfect for pinot. The surrounding mountains force heat onto the plains, and the winds that sweep down their steep sides keep the rainfall at bay. Cool nights give the grapes time to build on the flavours they have developed throughout the day.

Not that the region is a one-grape wonder. Chardonnay, pinot gris, gewürztraminer, riesling, chenin blanc and sauvignon blanc all

Ata Rangi

Palliser Estate

perform well in local conditions, and a couple of medal-winning sparkling wines have also been produced. Cabernet sauvignon and its mates, merlot and cabernet franc, are generally less successful, but a few good examples have been made by forcing the vines to produce less, concentrating flavour into the berries that are allowed to remain.

The Wairarapa was New Zealand's undisputed pinot noir champion for the first few years of its development, but recently Central Otago, Canterbury/Waipara and Marlborough have begun to challenge its supremacy. This is all to the good. Regional styles will emerge as winemakers fine-tune their products to take advantage of their particular local conditions, and that can only be of benefit to the whole country.

A visit to the Wairarapa is a rewarding experience. Martinborough is the obvious place to start, but there are many delights to be found in the satellite villages within an hour's radius of the town – and they're not all wine oriented. Goat's cheese, mushrooms, walnuts and many different fruits and vegetables are just some of the food delights produced by local enthusiasts.

But wine is the thing, and no matter where you end up, you will probably be near a vineyard. At the very least, there is certain to be a shop where Wairarapa wines are sold with pride. **VW**

Martinborough Vineyard

Martinborough Vineyard is on a mission to create the finest New World pinot noir, a somewhat challenging task it could be said. Nevertheless, their record of awards and international recognition as a premium producer of pinot noir and chardonnay certainly confirms they are on the right track.

Leaf plucking was in full swing when we arrived at Martinborough Vineyard. Selected leaves are removed by hand to expose the fruit to the sun and encourage the vine to put its efforts into the fruit. It is helpful to witness processes like this as they demonstrate the handcrafted aspect of winemaking in the vineyard.

Conversation moved to the subject of wine and food matching – always a fun debate. A good plan is to determine the subtle taste and textural characteristics of the wine, and match food to these. This full-flavoured duck casserole has layers of texture complementary to Martinborough's complex pinot noir – chorizo-spice infused creamy white beans, pull-apart duck and its crispy skin, the substance of the mushrooms and rich aromatics.

JLeC

Duck with white beans, chorizo & mushrooms

SERVES 4

3 tblsp olive oil
4 duck legs (drumstick and thigh)
4 cloves garlic, chopped
2 red onions, sliced
1 cup sliced button mushrooms
2 chorizo sausages, sliced
1/2 cup Martinborough Pinot Noir
3 large tomatoes, skinned and chopped
10g morels (dried exotic mushrooms) soaked in 1/2 cup warm water to soften
2 cups chicken stock
2 tblsp chopped fresh oregano
1 cup white haricot or baby lima beans, soaked overnight in plenty of cold water
1 bay leaf
sea salt and freshly ground black pepper

1 Heat a large ovenproof casserole, add oil and brown the duck legs on both sides, remove to one side. Add garlic, onions, mushrooms and chorizo sausage and cook for 2 minutes.
2 Add pinot noir, tomatoes, morels and their soaking liquid, stock, oregano, drained beans, bay leaf and duck legs. Bring to the boil, then cover and bake in oven preheated to 180°C for 1 hour.
3 Remove covering, season with salt and pepper to taste. Return to cook uncovered for a further 20–30 minutes to brown duck skin.

Recipe created by Julie Le Clerc

Wine: Martinborough Vineyard Pinot Noir

Pinot noir is a classic partner for duck. The meat has a natural sweetness that is picked up by the cherry/berry characters in the wine, and in this dish the link is made even more symbiotic by including a healthy dollop of wine in the cooking liquid. Mushrooms are another aromatic link, because good pinot often carries a vaguely fungal whiff.

Pinot may be Martinborough Vineyard's great challenge, but the other members of its portfolio are equally well respected. Chardonnay is treated to all the winery techniques that transform it from a relatively straightforward beverage to a complex glassful of aromas and flavours, and an opulent dessert riesling, made when conditions are favourable, has a cult following. **VW**

PALLISER ESTATE

Part of the story of Palliser's success lies in the landscape of Martinborough, one of the most exciting wine-producing regions in New Zealand. Palliser Estate vineyards are planted on alluvial terraces of loamy free-draining soil, an old river plain network surrounded by sun-baked hills. These natural qualities present grapes harvested with a high premium value, and the quality of Palliser grapes is acknowledged as among the best in New Zealand.

Low cropping levels tend to be produced by intrinsic, cool, windy spring weather. Reliable dry autumns increase the intense, undiluted flavours. These circumstances, naturally imposed by the weather here, tend to create the essential ingredients of power and concentration from which great wines are produced. Palliser's business is the production of ultra premium wines while treasuring this environment.

Both the food and wine featured are unique products of New Zealand. Whitebait are fished from Lake Ferry, although any New Zealand whitebait would be most acceptable in this frittata – a play on the ubiquitous whitebait fritter. **JLeC**

LAKE FERRY WHITEBAIT FRITTATA

SERVES 8

2 tblsp olive oil
2 onions, peeled and thinly sliced
500g fresh New Zealand whitebait
1/2 cup chopped fresh parsley
6 eggs, lightly beaten
sea salt and freshly ground black pepper
2 tblsp olive oil
lemon wedges to garnish

1   Pre-heat oven to 180°C.
2   Heat a pan, add oil and onions and cook over a gentle heat for 10 minutes until softened without colouring. Mix onions, whitebait, parsley and eggs together and season well with salt and pepper.
3   Heat second measure of oil in a 24cm ovenproof frypan, pour in mixture. Cook over a moderate heat for 2–3 minutes, stir mixture once. Place into oven and bake for 45 minutes or until set and golden brown.
4   Serve sliced with lemon wedges to squeeze over.

Recipe created by Julie Le Clerc

WINE: PALLISER ESTATE SAUVIGNON BLANC

Marlborough has made New Zealand sauvignon world-famous, but this aromatic grape also grows well in the Wairarapa. The local interpretation of the style tends to be less aggressive than its South Island cousin, and that makes it particularly good with seafood. Eggs are often cited as a difficult match for wine, but the inclusion of chopped onion and a generous amount of parsley in this recipe eliminates any potential problems.

Palliser Estate wines have achieved good medal success over the years. Unlike some Martinborough producers, the company doesn't place any more emphasis on pinot noir than on its other wines, and as a result enjoys a good reputation right across its range. Riesling and chardonnay are both well respected, and when weather conditions allow a dessert wine to join the ranks, it usually sells out within a few weeks. **VW**

WINSLOW WINES

Winslow is a successful low-profile winery, making its mark producing distinctive, quality wines. 'This wine embodies the vineyard,' says owner Steve Tarring of Winslow Turakirae Reserve, a blend of cabernet sauvignon and cabernet franc. Steve goes on to discuss brilliant combinations of food that would work a treat with this outstanding and complex red, such as rare meats when the wine is younger, because the protein is a good foil for the tannins. As the wine ages he recommends roast quail with soft polenta and herbs, plus a good drizzle of top-quality extra virgin olive oil.

A welcoming tasting room is adorned with personal touches and handcrafted masks, the symbol of the winery. Be sure to try the extra special treat of a fascinating cabernet-based liqueur, with rich fruit and spice flavours based on Steve's grandmother's memorable home-made Christmas mince pies. **JLeC**

Conventional wisdom has it that Martinborough is not the right place to grow cabernet sauvignon, but Steve and Jennifer Tarring are determined to prove the doubters wrong. They went a long way towards doing just that when their 1998 Turakirae Reserve Cabernet Sauvignon/Cabernet Franc won a gold medal at the International Wine and Spirit competition in London. But the Winslow story is not all about reds. The company has produced some startlingly good rieslings in the last couple of years, as well as an attractive cabernet-based rosé. A visit to their tiny cellar shop is a rewarding experience. **VW**

Margrain Vineyard

The Old Winery Café is a café-style eatery and small function facility attached to Margrain Winery and overlooking the old vines of what was the Chifney Estate. Here, a well-known local chef whips up appealing and tasty food to partner the excellent wines of Margrain, for which tasting notes are thoughtfully provided to diners. The menu card is aimed at clients who want a leisurely experience for brunch, lunch or dinner. The brunch dishes are gutsy and substantial, and signature dishes such as lamb's fry and calamari also feature along with excellent fresh salmon, plus accompaniments of great chutneys made on-site.

A tasting room is adjacent to the café for sampling and bottle sales. Downstairs is an atmospheric converted cellar space for intimate functions. As this room lies mostly below ground level, the only window is at head height, giving a unique view of the underside of the vine canopy. **JLeC**

Pumpkin, corn and feta fritters

MAKES 24 TO SERVE 6-8

4 eggs, separated
3/4 cup cream
420g can creamed sweetcorn
8 tblsp self-raising flour
1 tblsp sweet chilli sauce
1/4 cup chopped fresh herbs (parsley and chives)
1 1/2 cups finely grated raw pumpkin (loosely packed)
100g feta cheese
sea salt and white pepper
grilled bacon, Parkvale (local) mushrooms, baby tomatoes and chutney to serve

1 Mix egg yolks, cream, corn, flour, chilli sauce, herbs, and grated pumpkin together in a large bowl.
2 Whisk egg whites until fluffy and soft peaks hold their shape and fold into first mixture. Add feta carefully and season well with salt and white pepper. Refrigerate for 1–2 hours to firm.
3 Spoon fritters onto hot oiled frying pan and cook over medium heat for approximately two minutes on each side. It is worth testing one first to get the timing right.
4 Serve fritters layered with crispy bacon, topped with roasted baby tomatoes and with grilled local Parkvale mushrooms and a good dollop of fruit chutney on the side.

Recipe created by chef Peter Icke, The Old Winery Café

Wine: Margrain Pinot Gris

Pinot gris seems to have an affinity for both grains and salty foods, so it's a natural with the major ingredients in these fritters. The Margrain version is dry, but it has an impression of sweetness that goes well with the fruit chutney served as an accessory.

The small Margrain range includes a nicely controlled chardonnay and a concentrated pinot noir. Impressive rieslings have also been produced in a couple of different styles, and a ripe-fruited merlot shows pinot noir isn't the only red grape that can be coaxed to perform well in the Wairarapa. **VW**

Venison & lentil soup

SERVES 6

1/4 cup extra virgin olive oil

1 onion, finely diced

2 large carrots, peeled and finely diced

2 sticks celery, finely diced

400g can crushed tomatoes

1 cup Sabarot Puy lentils

1 bay leaf

1 cup Nga Waka Pinot Noir

3 cups beef or venison stock

300g Cervena/venison shortloin, finely diced

2 tblsp chopped fresh coriander or parsley

sea salt and freshly ground black pepper

1 Heat a large saucepan, add oil and cook onion, carrot and celery over medium heat for 10 minutes, stirring regularly. Stir in tomatoes, lentils, bay leaf, pinot noir and stock and bring to the boil. Reduce heat and simmer uncovered for 25 minutes.

2 Heat a frypan, add a little oil and quickly brown venison in batches. Add venison to soup and cook for 5 minutes more. Remove bay leaf. Purée half the mixture and return to the saucepan. Stir in coriander and season with salt and pepper to taste.

Recipe created by Julie Le Clerc

Wine: Nga Waka Pinot Noir

Stylish is the word for this wine. It's not a blockbuster, but that's not what good pinot is all about. Its appeal is in the nicely focused cherry and strawberry aromas, and the softness of its flavour profile. They are qualities that make it a natural partner for the sweetness and tenderness of top-quality farmed Cervena.

Nga Waka is a small producer with a well-deserved reputation for quality. Riesling, chardonnay and sauvignon blanc all feature good flavour intensity, but they also boast a measure of elegance. That's an impressive balancing act. **VW**

Nga Waka Vineyard

A passing sun shower deposits large droplets onto nodding vine leaves. The sound drums down onto the corrugated iron of the winery at Nga Waka. Whoever said picture books have to feature only fine weather? The water bestows a magical sparkle to the vines as the sun reappears above the three upturned canoe-shaped hills (representing waka, which are canoes, of the legendary Maori explorer Kupe) from which Nga Waka takes its name.

Nga Waka is a family concern, established to produce small volumes of consistently excellent wines that reflect the land with an intensity and depth of flavour typical of the Martinborough region. The winery buildings are of the 'designer New Zealand barn variety', very much at one with the countryside and epitomising a laid-back but uncompromising approach to quality winemaking. Nga Waka wines speak volumes. **JLeC**

Te Kairanga Wines

y River Wines

TE KAIRANGA WINES

Lovely old examples of classic MG cars cruised the highways and byways in and around Martinborough during our visit. There seemed to be some kind of MG convention in progress, and many of the car enthusiasts were also obviously wine enthusiasts because the cars converged on some of the best vineyards in the region, and the owners were seen sampling wine and enjoying the scenery.

Further out on the road from the town of Martinborough lie the established vines of Te Kairanga, a pretty country vineyard. Although it is one of the region's largest producers, Te Kairanga is still small by world standards. Te Kairanga is run by a team of skilled professionals, who are uncompromising in their strive for quality, and combine their demanding standards with a passion for wine and genuine Kiwi hospitality. As well as sampling and purchasing from the cheerful tasting room, visitors can enjoy 'walk, talk and taste tours' that demonstrate how the vineyard and winery operate. Wine-loving picnickers are also welcomed to this pleasant location. **JLeC**

Te Kairanga general manager, Andrew Shackleton, startled guests at the 2000 New Zealand Wine Society Royal Easter Wine Show when his company was presented with the 'Best Cabernet Sauvignon' award. 'Thanks,' he said, 'I'm delighted, of course, but we've just pulled the vines out!'

It was a surprise, but Andrew explained that the trophy winning 1998 wine was a 'once in a decade' effort. 'Most years, it's too hard to get cabernet properly ripe in Martinborough,' he told the audience.

Recent new plantings in the sprawling Te Kairanga vineyards have been dominated by pinot noir, but the company also places a lot of emphasis on chardonnay. Reserve versions of both wines are often outstanding, and a pleasantly approachable sauvignon blanc also has a keen following. **VW**

Gladstone Vineyard

Combine a drive in the countryside with a visit to Gladstone Vineyard. On weekends during the months of summer it is possible to stay and enjoy an alfresco lunch at the Gladstone Vineyard Café. Dine among the vines while enjoying the well-regarded wines. Outdoor seating is placed within a most beautiful setting of large established trees, a pond graced with an array of ducks and geese, a pétanque court and lush garden, all surrounded by the expansiveness of the vineyard.

The menu is summery and offers an unpretentiously small but inviting selection of dishes. Wonderfully appropriate vineyard platters also feature. Blackboard desserts vary daily, or you can simply opt for sampling excellent local cheeses with fruits and crackers. This is a welcoming place, and a bonus for family visits is that children are also well catered for. However, a pleading admonishment is given not to feed the sociable vineyard dogs – especially the big golden one!

JLeC

Warm salad of Greek lamb koftas

SERVES 4

1 cup fresh breadcrumbs
150 ml milk
675g minced lamb
2 tblsp grated or very finely chopped onion
3 cloves garlic, crushed
2 tsp ground cumin
2 tblsp chopped parsley
sea salt and freshly ground black pepper
flour for dusting
olive oil
dressed salad greens
sliced tomato, cucumber and red onion
1/2 cup plain yoghurt mixed with chopped fresh mint
1/4 cup toasted pinenuts

1   Mix the breadcrumbs with milk and leave to soak briefly.
2   Combine this with lamb, onion, garlic, cumin and parsley and mix well. Season with salt and pepper to taste.
3   Shape into little fat sausages. When ready to cook, toss in flour to lightly coat and shallow fry in a little olive oil.
4   To serve, place dressed salad greens, sliced tomato, cucumber and red onion into a deep plate. Top with the koftas, spoon minted yoghurt over the top and sprinkle with toasted pinenuts.

Recipe adapted by chef Miriam Williams, Gladstone Vineyard Café

Wine: Gladstone Sauvignon Blanc

Sauvignon blanc is a perfect match for the crisp, clean flavours of Greek cuisine, and in this dish it even stands up to the minted yoghurt – a challenge for any wine. The Gladstone Sauvignon Blanc has a brief spell in oak, and the gentle spiciness this brings to the palate ties in nicely with the seasoned lamb and toasted pinenuts.

The Gladstone white portfolio includes an attractive riesling, a pinot gris that in most years rewards short-term cellaring, and a middleweight chardonnay. Reds are less consistent, but in warm years the label is worn by a handful of rewarding blends based around cabernet sauvignon and merlot. **VW**

SUSAN

ATA RANGI
· MARTINBOROUGH ·

Gladstone Vineyard

Ata Rangi

From humble pioneering beginnings, Ata Rangi has risen incrementally to its present venerable status as a stellar New Zealand wine producer. Maybe the fact that four totally dedicated partners, three of them winemakers, own Ata Rangi contributes to the strong amount of personality present in the wines. The partners clearly demonstrate verve and commitment, and build sumptuous wines of depth and character. 'The best winemakers promote a strong connection between the vineyard and the winery,' observes Clive Paton, one of the owner/winemakers. This way 'the wine expresses the essence of the vineyard in the bottle'.

Note: Dukkah is a spice mixture of Egyptian origin but sometimes found in other parts of the Middle East. Rather like wine, each dukkah recipe shows the maker's personality, and varies from place to place and from family to family. Originally designed to be eaten dry as a dip for bread and olive oil, dukkah can also be used in cooking to enhance many dishes. The smoky, spicy, peppery characters harmonise particularly well with Ata Rangi's opulent blend, Célèbre, especially with the element of syrah. **JLeC**

LAMB RUMP WITH SPICY DUKKAH & OVEN-ROASTED TOMATOES

SERVES 4

DUKKAH:

1/4 cup sesame seeds, toasted
1 tblsp cumin seeds, toasted
2 tblsp coriander seeds, toasted
1/4 cup blanched almonds, toasted
2 tsp bittersweet La Chinata Spanish smoked paprika
1 tsp dried thyme, rubbed to a powder
1/2 tsp freshly ground black pepper
1 tsp sea salt
4 tomatoes, cut in half
basil or mint leaves
4 lamb hearts of rump

1 Toast seeds and nuts separately and grind together carefully so as not to turn into a paste. Mix in smoked paprika, thyme, pepper and salt. Store covered in the refrigerator but best used freshly made.

2 Place tomato halves onto a lightly oiled oven tray cut side up, season with salt and pepper and bake for 1 hour at 160°C until partially dried. Serve scattered with basil or mint.

3 Heat a pan, add oil and brown lamb on all sides. Roll in generous amounts of dukkah, place in an oven pan and roast for 15 minutes at 200°C. Remove to rest and keep warm for 10 minutes.

4 Slice lamb to serve with tomatoes on the side.

Recipe created by Julie Le Clerc

WINE: ATA RANGI CÉLÈBRE

The Célèbre blend varies from year to year, but it usually includes cabernet sauvignon, merlot, syrah and cabernet franc. It is a combination that presents several opportunities to interact with this dish – cabernet sauvignon and lamb are natural partners, merlot is good with tomatoes, and the spices find their ideal match in the syrah. Cabernet franc is a cousin of cabernet sauvignon and is said to add charm to any blend in which it is used, but it also seems to bring out the best in mint or basil.

Ata Rangi is best known for its pinot noir, an impeccably balanced wine that has won several awards in this country and overseas, but its family owners also produce a couple of excellent variations on the chardonnay theme. An opulently fruited pinot gris is beautifully made, but the level of sweetness it carries in most years makes it a difficult match for food. **VW**

Dry River Wines

Neil McCallum, owner and winemaker of Dry River Wines, says New Zealanders are reinventing the wheel by 'taking the passionate traditions of Europe in juxtaposition with analysis and scientifically managed evolution' to achieve production of the best examples of fine wines. Dry River's wines are quite extraordinary, with a developed style that focuses on quality, concentration and longevity.

Neil gave qualified direction that 'choucroute' has long been considered a classic match to off-dry riesling. With this in mind, it is not surprising that a revamped version, inspired by the time-honoured recipe of Alsaçe, works well with Dry River's magnificent riesling. Tongue tingling, vaguely tart and tangy/spicy, its salty qualities are a stimulating pairing with the pleasant citrus acidity of the wine. The red cabbage gives the whole dish a vibrant colour lift, but ordinary cabbage could also be used. **JLeC**

Red cabbage 'choucroute'

SERVES 4

1/2 small red cabbage, thinly sliced	10 juniper berries, lightly crushed by
1 tblsp salt	pounding
1 tblsp olive oil	1 cup Dry River Riesling
3 slices bacon, cut into thin strips	1 cooking apple, cored and thinly sliced
1 onion, peeled and finely sliced	2 tblsp cider vinegar
2 cloves garlic, chopped	sea salt and freshly ground black pepper
2 bay leaves	4 pork cutlets, trimmed

1   Place cabbage into a colander and sprinkle with 1 tblsp salt and leave for 1 hour. Rinse well.
2   Heat a large ovenproof casserole, add oil and cook bacon over a medium heat. Add onion and garlic and gently stir-fry for 5 minutes. Mix in prepared cabbage, bay leaves and juniper berries.
3   Add wine and enough cold water to just cover cabbage. Bring to the boil, cover and simmer very gently for 30 minutes. Now add the apple and vinegar and season with salt and pepper to taste. Cook for a further 10 minutes to soften apple.
4   Season pork with salt and pepper. Heat an ovenproof frying pan, add a little oil and brown pork cutlets on both sides, finish cooking in a preheated oven for 5–10 minutes at 180°C. Serve with red cabbage choucroute.

Recipe created by Julie Le Clerc

Wine: Dry River Riesling

Neil McCallum lets the grapes dictate the sweetness of his rieslings, but this dish works best with his off-dry versions. Fruit intensity is a Dry River trademark, and it enables the wine to sit comfortably alongside the outspoken flavours of ingredients like juniper berries and bacon. The natural sweetness ties in nicely with the pork, the crisp acids link up with the apple, and the long finish seems to tie everything together.

Dry River wines aren't entered in competitions, but they consistently win top ratings from respected commentators around the world. Every member of the portfolio is a standout, from a full-flavoured but elegant pinot gris to an impressively stylish pinot noir. Chardonnay, gewürztraminer, sauvignon blanc, syrah and a couple of dessert wines are all exceptional, and most sell out within days of release. **VW**

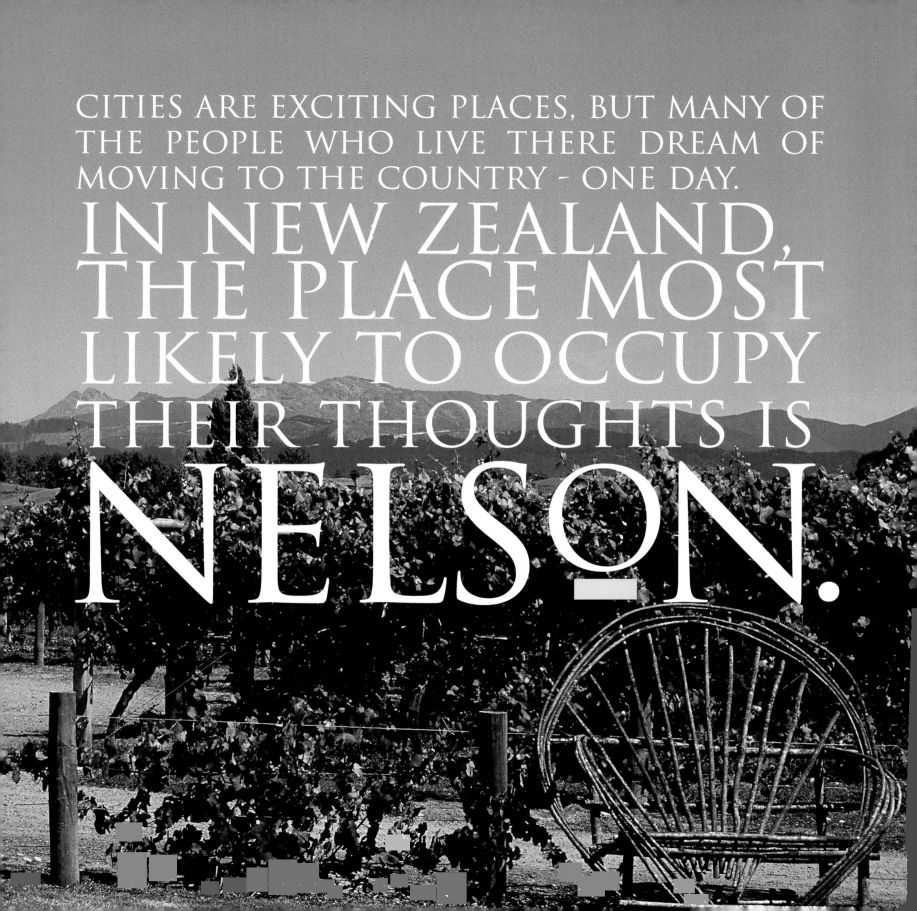

CITIES ARE EXCITING PLACES, BUT MANY OF THE PEOPLE WHO LIVE THERE DREAM OF MOVING TO THE COUNTRY - ONE DAY. IN NEW ZEALAND, THE PLACE MOST LIKELY TO OCCUPY THEIR THOUGHTS IS NELSON.

Neudorf vineyard

mouters hills

Moutere Hills Vineyard

Neudorf Vineyard

LONG-TIME HOME TO ARTISTS and craftspeople, Nelson is a picturesque region centred around a couple of pretty towns boasting a disproportionate number of cafés and restaurants.

Most years, it claims more sunshine hours than anywhere else in the country, usually just beating nearby Marlborough to the top slot. Autumn rain, drifting off the nearby mountains, can be a problem for the local grapes, but there's seldom enough to offer a serious threat.

The soil contains a high percentage of clay, which is why so many potters favour the area. Grape growers aren't quite so enthusiastic, but they say as long as it is reasonably friable it is still capable of producing excellent fruit.

Nelson has a reputation as white wine country, but that is selling it short. Certainly, riesling, chardonnay and sauvignon blanc have had the front-running for the last few years, but a number of top-notch pinot noirs have also been produced, and local hero Dave Glover is leading the charge to prove cabernet sauvignon can also perform well, providing its crops are restricted to force more flavour into the grapes.

The region's pioneers were Tim and Judy Finn, from Neudorf Vineyards, and Hermann and Agnes Seifried, from Seifried Estate. The Seifrieds run the only winery of any size in the area, and have enjoyed good medal success over the years. The Finns seldom enter competitions, but their wines, particularly chardonnay and pinot noir, enjoy an international reputation.

Spencer Hill Estate, Greenhough, Moutere Hills, Denton, Brightwater, McCashin's, Te Mania and Kahurangi Estate are among the other companies producing enough to send reasonable quantities around the country and overseas, but many local properties are so tiny their labels are seldom seen outside the area. **vw**

Denton Winery

It would be hard to find a prettier setting for a vineyard café than the situation at Denton Winery. A vineyard backdrop, park-like grounds and a flower garden make this an idyllic place to visit. Settle down and enjoy a bottle of wine with light, innovative food while relaxing on the terraces that overlook a water lily-filled lake. Much thought and care has been put into creating this charming place and likewise the food and wine. Warm and hospitable hosts, Richard and Alexandra Denton do everything right down to the last detail, as they themselves would like. There is a lingering impression that no one element makes the place – it is truly a combined experience.

The Denton menu-style exemplifies simplicity and top quality produce, combining excellent local cheeses, freshly baked bread, preserves beyond compare and fine wines, all made on the premises. Choices are uncomplicated and full of delightful surprises, such as Alexandra Denton's sublime spiced figs and a range of imaginative chutneys and jellies. **JLeC**

Mustard fruits

MAKES 2 LITRES

300g dried figs	1 cup water
300g dried New Zealand apricots	2 1/2 cups sugar
250g dried nectarines	4 tblsp whole grain mustard
200g dried pears	2 tsp yellow mustard seeds
200g dried pineapple pieces	1/2 cup lemon juice
1 litre cider vinegar or white wine vinegar	4 cloves garlic, crushed

1 Soak dried fruit in warm water for 1/2 hour, then rinse in cold water. Figs may need soaking for a little longer if they are particularly dry.
2 Place remaining ingredients into a large heavy-based stainless steel (not aluminium) pan. Bring to the boil then add dried fruits. Simmer gently until fruits are soft but still mostly whole. Some of the fruit may break down a little but this is fine.
3 To sterilise jars, wash and place in oven at 150°C for at least 1/2 hour (including lids).
4 Ladle mustard fruits into hot jars and seal securely.
5 Best kept for a few weeks before use. Refrigerate after opening. Great served with soft cheese such as local Evansdale Brie, blue cheese or ham and freshly baked bread.

Recipe created by Alexandra Denton

Wine: Denton Chardonnay

Which of the two Denton chardonnays you choose to accompany Alexandra's mustard fruits depends on the food they are to complement. With ham or other cold meats, the 'standard' version, with its upfront, citric characters would work well, but if your preference is for cheese and chunky bread, the bolder, richer Reserve version (Richard describes it as 'a symphony, rather than a soloist') would be more appropriate.

The Dentons are perfectionists, and it shows both in Alexandra's paintings (she is an accomplished artist) and Richard's wines. The flavour of every member of the range is clean and focused. Denton Sauvignon Blanc is invariably upfront and refreshing, and in most years the pinot noir is a fruit-led middleweight, and all the more appealing because of it. Merlot is a rarity in Nelson, and syrah even more so, but through careful winemaking Richard has made attractive and approachable wines from both varieties. **VW**

Smoked fish & mussel sandwich with garlic mayonnaise

SERVES 2 OR MORE IF YOU'RE NOT THAT HUNGRY – BUT YOU WILL BE WHEN YOU SEE IT!

1 small round focaccia bread (or similar equivalent)

300g freshly smoked fish (we use warehau from the Smokehouse in Mapua)

6 smoked mussels

1/2 cup Simon's garlic mayonnaise (see recipe below)

salad: whatever comes to hand – a lettuce leaf, 2 tomatoes, a few slices of cucumber and pepper, half a spring onion, 3 or 4 pitted Nelson olives and a couple of lemon wedges

1 Toast the bread in an oven at 180°C for 5 minutes or until the crust is crispy. Slice in half.
2 Spread mayonnaise generously over inner surfaces; fill sandwich with selected ingredients. Cut into two and serve with lemon wedges on the side.

SIMON'S GARLIC MAYONNAISE (MAKES 1 1/2 CUPS):

2 egg yolks (we use Moutere Hills' own free range eggs as they really do taste better)

1/4 cup white wine vinegar

3–4 cloves garlic, crushed

1 tsp whole grain mustard

pinch cayenne pepper

sea salt and freshly ground black pepper

1 cup canola oil (the flavour of olive oil is too strong in this instance)

1 Place egg yolks and vinegar into the mixing bowl or food processor and blend gently for 30 seconds. Add everything else except the oil and blend gently for another 30 seconds.
2 With the motor running or while whisking add oil drop-wise at first, slowly increasing the flow to a steady trickle until fully incorporated. Lasts about 2 weeks stored in the refrigerator.

Recipe created by Angela Kernohan and Simon Thomas, Moutere Hills Vineyard

Wine: Moutere Hills Nelson Sauvignon Blanc

Simon Thomas likes to get 'different' flavours into his sauvignon blancs, and in various vintages he has experimented with fermenting part of the juice in oak barrels, and leaving a little residual sugar in the final blend. The techniques add richness, soften the acids and make the wine less zingy than most. It is the smooth texture that makes it a good match for the garlic mayonnaise in this recipe – a livelier wine would have been too intrusive for the palate-coating egg yolks.

Besides the sauvignon blanc, the Moutere Hills range includes a meaty chardonnay, a sweetish riesling, a charming pinot noir and a couple of variations on the cabernet sauvignon/merlot theme. A super-sweet dessert wine is also made when weather conditions are suitable. **VW**

Moutere Hills Vineyard

While waiting for lunch, many visitors to Moutere Hills Vineyard follow the compelling sign suggesting 'a gentle stroll'. A short amble reveals a charming seating arrangement and an unequalled view over the countryside. A cacophony of cicadas fills the hot summer breeze, which has turned the grass the colour of caramel. Moutere Hills Sauvignon Blanc is also warmer, less green-grassy than some versions, and with a delightful toffee-caramel flavour, balanced with a fresh citrus finish. It picks up the vanilla butterscotch flavours from spending a short while in oak. This is a moreish summer wine, which is very compatible with a sandwich crammed full of the delights of the region. A local smokehouse at Mapua prepares succulent fish that in effect caramelises in the smoking process.

Moutere Hills is a character-filled place where great ingenuity has been used to adapt existing buildings into useful winery ones. The winery is in a converted wool shed; the shop was a hop kiln. This is very much a family affair where the warmth, friendliness and passion of the owners are palpable. **JLeC**

GLOVER'S VINEYARD

Settled in dramatic countryside, Glover's Vineyard has the wonderful, rustic charm that can only be found at smaller establishments. Personality-plus is imbued into the Glover wines, producing some very unique tastes and textures. This is a very personable set-up where many tasters are welcomed by the owner/winemaker, and often return again and again. While chatting to others in the tasting room at Glover's, one visitor on a regular personal wine tour of the region commented that 'all the local wineries are great but I like to save the best until last'. Such is the attraction to the sincerity of Glovers.

Dave Glover suggested scallops and grapefruit as the basis for a recipe to serve with his lighter-style late-harvest riesling, and this turned out to be an excellent combination. If celeriac is unobtainable, try celery, very thinly sliced. The refreshing crunch is a nice contrast to the richness of the scallops.

JLeC

SALAD OF NELSON SCALLOPS WITH RUBY GRAPEFRUIT AND CELERIAC

SERVES 4 AS A STARTER

1 small bulb celeriac (tuberous root vegetable with a mild celery-like flavour)
juice of 1 lemon
20 scallops, cleaned
1 ruby (pink) grapefruit, peel removed
2–3 tblsp orange-infused olive oil (I love the quality Colonna range of infused oils)
1/2 cup caper berries (the seedpods of the caper plant)
sea salt and freshly ground black pepper
2 tblsp chopped fresh coriander

1   Peel celeriac, slice thinly and cut slices into thin strips. Sprinkle with lemon juice and use as a base for scallops.
2   Heat a pan and sear scallops quickly on both sides in a little oil. Segment grapefruit and toss segments and juice with scallops, orange-infused oil and caper berries. Season with salt and pepper to taste and arrange on top of celeriac. Scatter over coriander to serve.

Recipe created by Julie Le Clerc

WINE: GLOVER'S RICHMOND RIESLING LATE HARVEST

'Pretty' is not a word that often comes to mind when tasting Dave Glover's wines, but it suits this one. The grapes were lightly affected by the (sometimes) beneficial mould, botrytis, and it has added a faintly savoury note that goes well with the coriander. The citric characters of grapefruit, lemon juice and orange-infused oil have an affinity for the riesling grape, and the scallops use their natural sweetness to link in with the same character in the wine.

Over the years, Dave Glover has spent a lot of time patiently explaining his approach to wine, particularly reds. He has been criticised for making them too tannic (his car number plate reads 'tannin'), but he is at pains to point out that he doesn't want this mouth-puckering characteristic for its own sake, but for the structure it adds to the flavour profile. His pinot noir and cabernet sauvignon-based reds are undoubtedly big and full of character, but many gain a surprising amount of finesse after a few years in a quiet spot. **VW**

NEUDORF
VINEYARDS

Moutere Hills Vineyard

SEIFRIED ESTATE

The Seifrieds have achieved a fine reputation for making stylish food-friendly wines, so establishing a restaurant and function centre at their estate was really a natural progression. The vineyard restaurant is open all year round. Here, delicious Seifried wine partners freshly prepared food, and the extensive menu has wine suggestions noted for each dish. The complex is situated in a peaceful rural setting, nestled among the French grapevines that thrive in the area's stony soils. The dining room leads onto a sunny courtyard garden and children's play area, so parents can relax and enjoy their meal.

The success of Seifried Estate's intense, handcrafted wines continues year after year. An extensive range is available for sampling in the complex's tasting area, and the cellar door is open daily. A warm and friendly welcome is assured. **JLeC**

Hermann and Agnes Seifried have done a huge amount to further the reputation of Nelson wines around the world. Their company is by far the largest in the region, and wines wearing their Seifried Estate and Old Coach Road labels are often the only local representatives on restaurant wine lists around the country. Hermann is particularly skilled with riesling and gewürztraminer grapes, but he has also made excellent wines from chardonnay and sauvignon blanc. His pinot noir is consistently one of the best-priced on the market, and when conditions make it possible to produce a dessert wine, it is invariably a standout. **VW**

Neudorf Vineyards

Neudorf Vineyards has the highest reputation for producing exceptional wines that reflect the assets of the region and the inimitable flair and subtlety of the winemaker. 'Great wines have a basis of fruit concentration and length – this occurs in the vineyard,' explains owner/winemaker Tim Finn. 'As a winemaker my job is to take the essence of the fruit and preserve it as wine – the aim is always to allow the site to be expressed through the fruit.'

Judy Finn tells of experiencing a 'magical unity' when drinking wine and eating food of a certain region, while actually being in that region. A parallel of geography turned into wine and food; the produce depicts the region. This wonderfully original recipe is therefore regionally perfect, made with Nelson's local Parkerfield chevre, although any strong, soft goat's cheese would do. Judy enjoys serving this soufflé with accompaniments of warm roasted eggplant and caramelised onions, and of course Neudorf's sensual, earthy Pinot Noir, which 'picks up all those lovely farmyard smells'.

JLeC

Goat's cheese soufflé

SERVES 6

6 day-old croissants
300g fresh soft goat's cheese, crumbled (the local Parkerfield chevre is excellent)
1/2 cup freshly grated Parmesan cheese
4 large eggs
2 tblsp Dijon mustard
3 cups milk
sea salt and freshly ground black pepper

1   Pre-heat oven to 175°C. Grease or spray a 20cm soufflé mould or baking dish with olive oil.
2   Tear each croissant into six pieces and place into soufflé dish. Scatter through goat's cheese and Parmesan.
3   In a bowl beat eggs until frothy. Add Dijon mustard and milk and blend well to combine. Season with salt and pepper. Pour over croissants and cheese and leave to soak in for 10 minutes. Bake in middle of oven for 50 minutes. Serve immediately.

Recipe supplied by Judy Finn

Wine: Neudorf Moutere Pinot Noir

Tim and Judy Finn make a trio of pinots – one, labelled 'Nelson', uses fruit from a couple of different sites, but this one and a 'reserve' version, made in exceptional years, are both sourced from the home vineyard. Judy chose the 2000 vintage to accompany her soufflé. Goat's cheese, served unadorned, is often partnered with sauvignon blanc because the variety's keen acids counteract the saltiness of the cheese. This match relies on different qualities for its success. The wine is elegant, with understated power, and the same could be said for the soufflé. The basic flavours sit together well, but the final link is provided by the touch of assertive Parmesan.

Neudorf wines are produced in tiny quantities, but they enjoy a world-wide reputation. The range includes a zesty sauvignon blanc, a charming riesling and a beautifully constructed chardonnay that shares the pinot's ability to hide its power behind an elegant first impression. **VW**

MARLBOROUGH IS NEW ZEALAND'S LARGEST WINEMAKING REGION, AND IT HAS ALMOST SINGLE-HANDEDLY BROUGHT THE LOCAL INDUSTRY TO THE ATTENTION OF THE WORLD

Steveson Estate

Wairau River Wines

CLOUDY BAY

CELLAR DOOR OPEN

Timara Lodge

JUST ONE GRAPE DESERVES THE KUDOS. Marlborough sauvignon blanc has been called the first totally new wine style of the past 100 years. This super-aromatic variety, until the 1980s best known in France's Sancerre district, has found a second spiritual home on the sun-baked plains at the top of the South Island. It thrives on the stone-covered river flats, growing flavour strength through the long, sunny days and consolidating during the crisp, cool nights.

Even the super-parochial French acknowledge that the zesty local style is the way of the future – locals are getting used to seeing Sancerre producers touring the region, cheque-books in hand, in search of land.

Marlborough sauvignon blanc is unique and exciting, but this much-blessed region is suitable for a wide range of grapes. Riesling, chardonnay, pinot noir, gewürztraminer, sémillon and pinot gris all perform well, and even hard-to-please cabernet sauvignon and its cellarmates, merlot and cabernet franc, can be coaxed along to give reasonably rich flavours. At Fromm, Hatsch Kalberer has broken all the rules with a series of intense reds based not only on these so-called Bordeaux varieties, but also on malbec and syrah – both grapes said to need baking heat to thrive.

Marlborough is also the centre of the nation's sparkling wine production. Industry giant, Montana, works with the house of Deutz in Champagne to make a local interpretation of their style, and even internationally famous Cloudy Bay takes a break from bottling the world's best-known sauvignon blanc to produce its own bubbly, Pelorus. Neither company enters its wines in local competitions, but many other Marlborough labels have achieved medal success.

Pinot noir is Marlborough's new red star. Very good wines have been produced from this notoriously finicky grape, and most sell for several dollars less than their stellar cousins in Martinborough, Waipara and Central Otago.

Visitors are often surprised to learn that wine grapes weren't planted seriously in the region until the early 1970s. Frank Yukich, then head of Montana Wines, had been told he was crazy to establish a vineyard on the Wairau Valley's dry, drought-prone soil, but that just encouraged him. He must be laughing now.

Marlborough's secret is in its stones. The whole valley was once crisscrossed with meandering rivers, and the stones the water left behind now reflect the sun's warmth onto the ripening grapes. That heat hangs around – an hour after sunset, the stones are still warm to touch, giving the grapes a little extra ripening time each day.

In the last few years, a second region has opened up in the Awatere Valley, a short drive from Blenheim. Here it is even drier and warmer than the Wairau, which is why several major companies have joined local growers in planting grapes. With land near any of Marlborough's big name properties now commanding a premium, it can be expected that sub-regions will continue to be discovered.

On the food side of the ledger, two winemaking couples deserve special mention. Toni and Terry Gillan have opened restaurants, shopping centres and a hotel in Blenheim since they arrived from the UK many years ago, and they have always had a good understanding of the place of honest food with good wine. Today, their cellar door sells tapas (Spanish nibbles) to go with their carefully made products.

More recently, Hans and Therese Herzog arrived from Switzerland, where they operated a Michelin-starred restaurant, and have established a winery, restaurant and tasting facility the likes of which the town has never seen. Many of the staff, including both chefs, have been brought over from Europe, and the wine list offers some of the world's greatest labels. Hans's own wines are a shining advertisement for low cropping, such is their intensity. **VW**

SERESIN ESTATE

From the entrance to the property, 'hands' guide visitors past expanses of vines to the winery. The distinctive handprint symbol of Seresin Estate is branded onto bollards along the driveway. 'The image of the hand is a symbol of strength, gate to the heart, tiller of the soil, mark of the artisan, and embodies the philosophy of Seresin Estate,' reads the company's brochure.

Part of this philosophy encompasses hosting unique food and wine events, including singularly extraordinary dinners held in a once disused boat-shed, hidden in the magnificent Marlborough Sounds, and stunningly transformed into a dining space. Guests are transported by boat, welcomed at the jetty and treated to a series of exquisite courses paired with the very sexy Seresin wines. One such magical dinner, with food cooked by the inimitable Peter Gordon, inspired this recipe. The shiveringly fresh riesling has a steely focus and definitive fruit character. This is a liquid essay in purity, which truly exemplifies Seresin Estate, wine of passion, grace and spirit. **JLeC**

SCALLOPS WITH LIME & GINGER CHILLI JAM

LIME & GINGER CHILLI JAM: MAKES 1 CUP

3 tblsp olive oil
1 large onion, sliced
3 cloves garlic, crushed
2 tblsp grated fresh ginger
6 large chillies, seeds removed and sliced
1 tblsp tomato paste
3/4 cup Seresin Riesling
finely grated zest of 2 limes
juice of 3 limes
1/2 cup soft brown sugar, tightly packed
sea salt to taste
extra limes, sliced

1 Heat a saucepan, add oil, onion, garlic and ginger. Cook over medium heat for 3 minutes, stirring until onion has softened.
2 Add remaining ingredients and bring to the boil, stirring until sugar has dissolved. Simmer for 15–20 minutes until thick and pulpy. Remove to cool.
3 Blend in a food processor until smooth.
4 Serve a small amount of jam on top of lightly seared scallops with extra lime on the side.

Recipe created by Julie Le Clerc, inspired by Peter Gordon

WINE: SERESIN RIESLING

Scallops and riesling form a magical combination, and this match is made all the more successful through the echoing of the wine's natural citric character by the lime zest in the jam. The glass of wine with which the zest is cooked consummates the marriage.

Brian Bicknell is a talented winemaker with a very clear idea of the styles he wants to create, and he has had notable success with chardonnay, sauvignon blanc, pinot gris, pinot noir, sparkling wine and even malbec – not a variety that, on the face of it, should do well in Marlborough. His secret is low cropping. Vines that have had some of their fruit removed just when it starts to ripen force all the flavour they can muster into the bunches that remain, and that intensity is reflected in the finished wine. **VW**

CELLIER LE BRUN

In the style of the Champagne region of France, the Cellier Le Brun winery is carved into a slope of land to create underground cellars – a naturally chilled storage area for ageing wine. Cellier Le Brun makes a small range of still wines, but specialises in producing a full range of Méthode Traditionnelle sparkling wines. Brut Taché has a pink sparkle and fruit expression from the addition of pinotage after disgorging. This colouring works beautifully to give the poached pears a delicate shade of blush.

The Terrace Café at Le Brun is a stylish restaurant positioned with a view to the vines and, for dinner guests, the possibility of an intense sunset. Breakfast and lunch are served inside or out in the courtyard, and this is a good time to try one of their famous platters. Dinners are limited to the end of the week. Be sure to save room for a dessert such as this sexy combination! **JLeC**

PANNACOTTA WITH POACHED PEARS

SERVES 6

2 leaves gelatine
1/2 cup milk
1 3/4 cups cream
2 tblsp sugar
1 vanilla pod, split lengthways
finely gated zest of 1/2 lemon
1/4 cup white rum
star anise and bay leaves to decorate

1 Place gelatine in a bowl with milk to soak and soften.
2 Combine 1 cup of the cream, sugar, split vanilla pod and lemon zest in a saucepan and bring almost to the boil. Remove from heat and strain onto softened gelatine and milk, stirring to dissolve completely. Add rum and leave to cool to room temperature.
3 Whip remaining cream to soft peaks and gently fold into cooled mixture. Pour into 6 greased 1/2-cup capacity moulds. Refrigerate overnight to set.
4 Dip moulds briefly into hot water and turn out onto serving plates. Serve with poached pears drizzled with syrup. Decorate with star anise and bay leaves.

POACHED PEARS:

2 cups Daniel Le Brun Taché
2 cups sugar
6 star anise

3 bay leaves
peeled zest of 1 lemon
6 firm pears, peeled to retain stalks

1 Combine first 5 ingredients in a saucepan and bring to the boil then reduce to a simmer. Add pears, cover with a piece of baking paper and poach until just tender. Allow to cool in syrup.

Recipe created by chef Simon Atkinson, Terrace Café at Le Brun

WINE: DANIEL LE BRUN BRUT TACHÉ MÉTHODE TRADITIONNELLE

This match was inspired by the wine's colour, but it is the flavours of the component parts that make it work. The dish is sweeter than the wine, which is usually a 'no-no', but the sugar is counteracted by the lemon juice and the cutting flavour of the star anise.

The Cellier Le Brun range is dominated by sparkling wines, but the company also produces a group of reds and whites under the Terrace Road label. **VW**

Cloudy Bay

Highfield Estate

SCOTT
WINES AND ESTATES LTD

Waterfall Bay

1998
CHARDONNAY RESERVE
MARLBOROUGH
NEW ZEALAND

1999
PINOT NOIR
MARLBOROUGH
NEW ZEALAND

Waterfall Bay

Lamb shanks with plums and oranges

SERVES 4–6

6–8 lamb shanks, knuckle removed

2 oranges, skins removed and sliced

1 onion, diced

6 cloves garlic, chopped

2 tblsp whole grain mustard

4 sprigs fresh rosemary

1 litre orange juice

400g can dark plums in syrup, drained

sea salt and freshly ground black pepper

1 Place lamb shanks into a deep non-reactive dish and cover with remaining ingredients, except plums. Make sure shanks are covered in liquid; top up with orange juice if necessary. Leave to marinate overnight.

2 Heat oven to 180°C. Transfer shanks and marinade to an ovenproof dish and cover with a tent of foil to allow for shanks to expand during cooking. Bake for 4 hours.

3 Remove shanks to rest in a warm place, covered in foil. Strain liquid, place in a saucepan and boil to reduce to 2 cups. Remove stones from plums. Roughly chop plums and add to saucepan. Continue to simmer to heat plums and further reduce sauce. Season with salt and pepper to taste.

4 Serve 1–2 lamb shanks per person with a generous amount of sauce.

Recipe created by chef Jennifer Mahoney, Hunter's Vintner's Restaurant

Wine: Hunter's Pinot Noir

Lamb is a natural partner for pinot, and a plum-like character is easy to find in the Hunter's interpretation of this approachable variety. The orange juice presents a challenge for the wine, but long, slow cooking marries it in with the other flavours.

The Hunter's label and Jane Hunter herself have done a tremendous amount to build and enhance the reputation of New Zealand wine overseas. The company has won countless international awards, and its wines are sold all over the world. In addition to this softly spoken pinot, Gary Duke makes stylish riesling and gewürztraminer, understated chardonnay, oaked and unoaked versions of sauvignon blanc and a couple of nicely balanced sparkling wines. **VW**

Hunter's Wines

Geography, climate, talent and strong determination contribute to the outstanding success of Hunter's Wines. 'When it's your name on the bottle the quality of the wine inside is a very personal thing,' says owner Jane Hunter OBE. Hunter's is highly regarded for producing top quality wines with tremendous varietal character.

Hunter's Vintner's Restaurant is open year round for lunch and dinner, and offers the enjoyment of their premium wines and warm hospitality. The restaurant has many charming features, including an outdoor dining area set in a lush garden, complete with a swimming pool for a cooling dip before lunch. The super-sized barbecue arrangement is spectacular, and must certainly streamline catering for a crowd. The superb meals are prepared with care, and feature Marlborough's renowned gourmet produce. Savour the flavours of this bountiful region. **JLeC**

ALLAN SCOTT WINES

Twelve Trees, the restaurant at Allan Scott Wines, is very tastefully arranged around a glorious garden setting. The restaurant was christened Twelve Trees after the twelve original walnut trees that lined the entrance road to the building, although a few have since disappeared. An appealing floral courtyard and prolific culinary garden lead onto yet another garden space that is prettily manicured and filled with a giant chessboard. Yes, a life-sized chessboard! Constructed of paving slabs and edged with herbs, full-sized chess pieces are literally picked up by the players and moved when a game is in action.

Lunches are served daily from a menu showcasing the produce of Marlborough. Excellent wine recommendations are given on the menu, creating discussion and a strong bond between the kitchen and the winemakers. **JLeC**

MARLBOROUGH GREENSHELL MUSSELS WITH PERNOD & CREAM

SERVES 2

1 cup Allan Scott Sauvignon Blanc
2 cloves garlic, peeled and chopped
1/2 small onion, roughly chopped
30 Marlborough Greenshell mussels, cleaned
2 tblsp Pernod
1/2 cup cream
1 red pepper, seeds removed, finely diced
2 tblsp snipped chives
sea salt
lemon wedges
fresh dill
sliced French bread

1 Place wine, garlic and onion into a large saucepan and bring to the boil. Add mussels, cover and steam for 1–2 minutes until mussels open. Remove to a serving bowl.
2 Strain wine and discard flavourings. Return wine to a saucepan and bring to the boil. Cook to reduce by half. Add Pernod and cream and reduce by half again. Add diced pepper and chives and salt to taste. Pour sauce over mussels. Garnish with lemon wedges, dill and serve with French bread to mop up the juices.

Recipe created by chef Robert Vanweers, Allan Scott Wines

WINE: ALLAN SCOTT SAUVIGNON BLANC

It's easy to see why the Twelve Trees team chose sauvignon blanc to accompany this dish – the wine's natural acids sit perfectly with the cutting character of Pernod. But that is just the start. Sauvignon is the ultimate shellfish wine, and matches always take on an extra dimension when everything on the table comes from the same region. In this case, Greenshell mussels and assertive sauvignon blanc are the two classic flavours of Marlborough.

Allan Scott, widely known as 'Scotty', is one of the Marlborough originals, having worked as a viticulturist for a couple of the largest local companies before establishing his own label. He makes a consistently good range that includes riesling, pinot noir, chardonnay, sparkling wine and, unusually in this region, cabernet sauvignon. A couple of dessert wines, made when conditions were favourable, have been standouts. **VW**

Beef fillet poached in pinot noir with Caesar salad

SERVES 12

1 bottle of Highfield Pinot Noir

3 star anise

1 1/4 cups beef stock

bouquet of fresh herbs (we have been
using lovage and lemon thyme)

2kg premium beef tenderloin eye fillet,
trimmed

sea salt and cracked peppercorns

1 Place all ingredients, except beef, into a large stainless steel saucepan and bring to the
boil. Simmer for 15 minutes then season with salt and cracked pepper. Add prepared fillet
of beef. Bring back to boil and simmer rapidly for 5 minutes.

2 Remove from the heat, cover tightly and leave undisturbed for 35 minutes. This process
will bring the beef to medium rare.

3 The beef can then be served warm or chilled, sliced and topped with Caesar salad.

CAESAR SALAD DRESSING:

2 egg yolks

1 clove garlic

1 tsp dry mustard

2 tsp sugar

pinch cayenne pepper

a few drops Tabasco sauce

1 cup olive oil

juice of 1/2 lemon

1 tblsp chopped chives

1 Place egg yolks, garlic, mustard, sugar, cayenne and Tabasco into the bowl of a food
processor; with the motor running, slowly add oil. Lastly blend in lemon juice and chives.

TO ASSEMBLE SALAD:

In a large bowl put 2 tblsp Caesar dressing, add cooked diced bacon, toasted croûtons,
2 tblsp of shredded Parmesan, and torn cos lettuce leaves as required. Toss well to coat
all ingredients with dressing.

Recipe created by chef Judith Steele, Highfield Estate

Wine: Highfield Pinot Noir

One way to increase the symbiotic relationship between plate and glass is to use some of the
wine in the pot, as chef Judith Steele has done here. But there is more to the match than that.
Star anise has a sweet-savoury quality that suits pinot, and the smokiness of the bacon in the
salad echoes the charred interior of the barrels in which the wine was matured.

Highfield covers the usual Marlborough range with an aromatic sauvignon blanc, an
approachable riesling and an elegant chardonnay, but their selection also includes a big but
stylish sparkling wine and a merlot that can be very good in warmer years. **VW**

Highfield Estate

Climb the tower of the Tuscan-castle
inspired Highfield Estate building to
revel in breathtaking panoramic views.
Highfield's distinctive structure stands
out in the countryside, and indeed
the countryside is outstanding from
the building. Undulating rows of
grapevines stretch out in all directions,
touched by a brilliant Marlborough sun.

Descend to dine indoors or pick a spot
on the expansive terrace. The Highfield
menu is concise, with a good selection
of varied and interesting choices,
promoting where possible organic and
regional foods. Thought is taken in the
approach of 'cooking to wine', that is,
understanding a wine first and then
designing food to complement it.
The blend of tastes and multiple
textures in a cleverly designed dish
such as beef fillet poached in pinot
noir with Caesar salad is multi-layered
and, combined with Highfield's pinot
noir, shows the different aspects of the
wine beautifully. **JLeC**

127

Vavasour Wines

Vavasour Wines can be found on the banks of the Awatere River in Marlborough. Here, using premium Awatere Valley grapes and selecting from the best of modern and traditional techniques, stylish wines are created with an elegance and subtlety that is uniquely Vavasour. This is a small family-based company with character – the distinctive cockerel on the wine labels is drawn from the Vavasour family crest, which dates back to 1066.

Winemaker Glenn Thomas says he really enjoys making riesling, and that in a way 'making riesling here is a kind of self indulgent thing' because only a small amount is produced. Great care is taken in handling the grapes to retain the fine aromatics, and the resulting wine is very sleek. The finish is long, crisp and dry. Vavasour riesling rewards cellaring, and can be thoroughly enjoyed with food. **JLeC**

Lime-roasted salmon & cavatelli pasta salad

SERVES 6

800g fresh salmon fillet, fine pin bones removed
juice and finely grated zest of 2 limes
1 tblsp brown sugar
sea salt and freshly ground black pepper
1 1/2 cups cavatelli pasta (my favourite – a light and delicate gnocchi-shaped pasta)
 or equivalent
3 tblsp Colonna lemon-infused olive oil
2 cloves garlic, crushed
1/2 cup finely diced gherkins
1/4 cup chopped fresh coriander
juice and finely grated zest of 2 limes
lime wedges to garnish

1 Pre-heat oven to 200°C. Place salmon skin side down into a roasting dish. Drizzle over lime juice, sprinkle over zest and brown sugar and season with salt and pepper. Roast for 10–15 minutes, depending on thickness of flesh, salmon should be cooked to medium rare. Allow to cool. Once cold break up flesh into good-sized pieces, discarding skin.

2 Cook pasta in plenty of boiling salted water for 8–10 minutes until tender, drain. Rinse under running cold water to cool. Drain well, toss in lemon-infused oil to prevent sticking together. Stir in garlic, gherkins, coriander, lime juice and zest, and season with salt and pepper to taste.

3 Gently mix salmon into prepared salad. Arrange on serving platter and garnish with lime wedges.

Recipe created by Julie Le Clerc

Wine: Vavasour Awatere Valley Riesling

Winemaker Glenn Thomas has an ability to get every last nuance of flavour from his grapes, and his wines are impressively focused as a result. Most years he leaves just a touch of residual sugar in his riesling, but not enough to kick it out of the 'dry' category. It is that touch of fruitiness that makes the wine such a good match for the sugar-infused salmon.

Vavasour Riesling has a keen following, but the company is probably better known for a very stylish chardonnay. The portfolio also includes sauvignon blanc that boasts more richness than many of the genre, a serious pinot noir and, in some years, a cabernet sauvignon that leans to leafiness in its youth but ages surprisingly well. A second range of wines is sold under the Dashwood label. **VW**

Framingham Wine Company

Framingham is one of Marlborough's oldest and most successful vineyards, sited on free-draining river gravel formed by the Wairau River over the centuries. This soil, coupled with Marlborough's unique climate, results in wine of unsurpassed intensity and flavour. Marlborough wines are loved for their youth and exuberance, and the innovative Framingham style captures this creative energy.

Framingham has a solid commitment to producing aromatic wines with outstandingly fresh fragrance and flavour. This strikingly well-balanced, late harvest riesling has the unusual addition of chenin blanc for the 2000 vintage. It shows nice apricot and honey flavours associated with the so-called 'noble rot', botrytis, that will turn to spice with age.

Note: Panpepato is a concentrated honey and spice, fruit and nut bread. Predecessor of the better known Tuscan panforte, its name comes from the surprising addition of a considerable amount of aromatic ground black pepper. **JLeC**

Panpepato

MAKES 2 SMALL LOAVES

1/2 cup muscatel raisins, soaked in 3 tblsp Late Harvest Riesling overnight
1 cup blanched almonds, toasted and roughly chopped
1/2 cup walnuts or hazelnuts, toasted and roughly chopped
1/2 cup pine nuts, lightly toasted
1/4 cup Dutch process cocoa powder
1/2 cup candied orange peel, chopped
1/2 tsp each ground cinnamon, nutmeg
1 tsp ground black pepper
1/2 cup liquid honey
1 cup plain flour
2 sheets edible rice paper

1 Pre-heat oven to 160°C.
2 Place all ingredients together into a bowl and mix well. Moisten hands with water and shape mixture into 2 round loaves. Place rice paper onto an oven tray or lightly grease an oven tray with olive oil if rice paper is unobtainable. Place loaves onto rice paper or prepared oven tray and bake for 30 minutes. Remove to cool completely.
3 Dust with extra cocoa powder and serve cut into small slices.

Recipe created by Julie Le Clerc

Wine: Framingham 2000 Late Harvest Riesling/ Chenin Blanc

It seems likely that this is the first time these two varieties have been blended together, but it may not be the last – it works brilliantly! Chenin has naturally high acid that counteracts riesling's exuberance, and picks up on the savoury flavours in the loaf.

Framingham owners, the Brooke-Taylors, sold their grapes to other companies for many years, but they have enjoyed considerable competition success since they have had their own label. Recent extra plantings will make them one of the larger players in the area. They enjoy an excellent reputation for riesling, but the range also includes sauvignon blanc, pinot gris, gewürztraminer, chardonnay, sparkling wine, merlot and a rare syrah. There are no duds. **VW**

Montana Brancott Winery

Framm Winery

Witner Hills Vineyard

Cloudy Bay

FROMM WINERY

The team at Fromm Winery is strongly focused on red wine production, believing that Marlborough has a huge potential for reds. They use labour intensive methods and care for the vines in a natural way to encourage this potential. Although first and foremost a red wine producer, with Pinot Noir as their flagship, Fromm's high quality white wines should certainly not be overlooked. All of Fromm's wines are sold under the brand name 'La Strada', which translates to 'the way' or 'the road' – a symbolic interpretation for the owners.

From the road, rows of vines stretch up towards the surrounding ranges. Yet another form of bird deterrent is evident at Fromm Winery – the trellises are arranged with laced strings of yellow plastic fluttering in the wind like the ribbons of rhythmic gymnasts. This method seems to be doing the trick in shooing birds away, and has the added bonus of attracting attention from humans. **JLeC**

Fromm Winery's Hatsch Kalberer has never been a follower of vinous fashion, and he has found two soulmates in winery owners, Georg and Ruth Fromm. Conventional wisdom has it that pinot noir is the only red grape suited to Marlborough's sunny day/cool night climate, but Fromm has blown that theory apart with a series of startlingly intense reds based on merlot, malbec and syrah. The secret, according to Hatsch, is a lot of extra time spent in the vineyard, pulling leaves away from the bunches and thinning the crop. It certainly pays off – Fromm reds aren't easy to find, but they're definitely worth the effort. Not into big reds? Try the beautifully tuned rieslings, made most years in both sweet and dry variations, and the intense but elegant chardonnay. **VW**

Journey through Marlborough platter

MARINATED MUSSELS:

1 dozen Marlborough Greenshell mussels

1/4 cup Deutz Marlborough Cuvée NV

1 tsp sweet chilli sauce

1 tsp oyster sauce

1 tsp soya sauce

1 clove garlic, finely chopped

1 tblsp olive oil

1. Place mussels and Deutz Marlborough Cuvée NV into a saucepan over heat. Steam to open; remove mussels from shells.
2. Combine remaining ingredients and mix with mussels to coat thoroughly. Place mussels back in half shells and serve on a mixed platter.

OLIVE DIP (MAKES 1 CUP)

1/2 cup black olives, pitted

2 tblsp chopped sundried tomatoes

2 tblsp freshly grated Parmesan cheese

4 anchovy fillets

2 cloves garlic, peeled

1/2 cup sour cream

sea salt and freshly ground black pepper

1. Combine all ingredients except sour cream in food processor. Blend until smooth. Fold in sour cream and season to taste with salt and pepper. Chill to serve.

Recipes created by chef Julie Robinson, Brancott Winery

Wine: Deutz Marlborough Cuvée NV

Méthode Traditionnelle is a versatile wine style that can be enjoyed any time of the day – even at breakfast! This big-selling example, made with considerable input from the House of Deutz in Champagne, has a depth of flavour that makes it a good match for the brashness of Marlborough mussels, even when they are combined with assertive extras like garlic, chillies and oyster sauce.

The giant Brancott Estate winery complex is Montana's Marlborough showcase. The tutored tastings are informative and enjoyable, and often include not only wines from other parts of the country, but also the products Montana distributes on behalf of other producers here and overseas. **VW**

Montana Brancott Winery

Montana is the largest winery in the Marlborough region. This is an outstanding space incorporating a retail store, tasting rooms, wine education centre, large restaurant with indoor and courtyard seating and children's playground. Here, there is something for everyone.

A bonus for visitors is the wine education facility. Informative audio-visual displays are presented along with interactive tastings and 'smelling' sessions.

The restaurant has an eclectic and ever-changing menu, and offers dishes featuring many distinctive flavours of the region. Nibbling items from a harvest platter is like taking 'a journey through Marlborough', and equally full of evocative sights, tastes and memories. **JLeC**

WITHER HILLS VINEYARD

While strolling among the vines, Brent Marris, inspired winemaker at Wither Hills, talks of creating wines in the vineyard, thus allowing the grapes to tell their own story. The fruit is the hero in his wines, and their essence depicts this remarkable region. Brent was brought up in this area so personally understands it very well. From this deep awareness he declares, 'All of Marlborough is in this wine – blue sky, green grass and cold water.' With a strong sense of purpose and vision, Brent Marris strives to capture this purity of flavour in his wines. He achieves wines that manifest harmony, a quality that makes them very easy to pair with food.

Plans are underway to build an integrated winery complex on the estate, the design of which is also very much in accordance with the region and the quality focus of Wither Hills. **JLeC**

OYSTERS WITH LEMON CAPER & PARSLEY SAUCE

SERVES 4

2 dozen oysters in the shell
crushed ice or rock salt
1 clove garlic, peeled
1 tblsp capers, drained
1/4 cup parsley leaves
1/4 cup extra virgin olive oil
3 tblsp Wither Hills Sauvignon Blanc
sea salt and freshly ground black pepper
1/4 red pepper, very finely diced
lemon wedges to serve

1 Remove any grit from the oysters and arrange on a serving platter with crushed ice or rock salt underneath to stabilise the shells.
2 In the bowl of a food processor purée garlic, capers and parsley together. With the motor running, drizzle in olive oil and wine to form a dressing. Season with salt and pepper to taste.
3 Spoon dressing over oysters and garnish with diced pepper. Serve with lemon wedges.

Recipe created by Julie Le Clerc

WINE: WITHER HILLS SAUVIGNON BLANC

Brent Marris's beautifully balanced sauvignon blanc has achieved near-cult status in New Zealand and overseas in a very short time. It is hardly surprising. The wine achieves the directness of aroma and flavour that has made the local style internationally famous, but behind that brash first impression it has layers of depth and complexity.

In the American city of Boston, an annual competition is held to determine the best wine to accompany oysters. When it was held for the first time a couple of years ago, 483 wines were entered from around the world. When the bags were pulled off the bottles, five of the top ten choices, including the first, second and third place-winners, were sauvignon blanc from Marlborough. Obviously, this is the ultimate oyster wine! The extras on the dish above enhance the match – red peppers, capers, garlic and parsley are all perfect with this aromatic variety.

A chardonnay and a pinot noir complete the Wither Hills range. Both display the immaculate balance that makes the sauvignon blanc such an instantly attractive drink. **VW**

Cloudy Bay

Legend has it that the Tahitian explorer Kupe arrived in the Marlborough Sounds and dredged the depths of Cloudy Bay for oysters. He used a scoop net, referred to by local Maori as 'Te Koko', to lift the oysters from the seabed. Following this adventure, the bay was originally called Te Koko-o-Kupe – the oyster dredge of Kupe. The legend lives on today in an adventurous wine from Cloudy Bay.

Te Koko is an individual expression of the sauvignon blanc grape released as a matured wine. The creative result of 'winemaking curiosity', the wine is fermented with naturally occurring yeast, followed by full malolactic fermentation, then left to age in barrels in contact with the yeast lees left over from fermentation. This is an extreme wine with loads of savoury flavour and 'rich in the mouth' texture, and is totally different from its internationally famous cellarmate. Te Koko is bold but user-friendly and very much a wine styled for food, with an ability to stand up to richer seafood better than the 'straight' version. **JLeC**

Prawn Salad with Toasted Pine Nut Dressing

SERVES 4

16–20 prawn cutlets, veins removed
200g bocconcini (small balls of mozzarella)
1/4 cup salted capers, soaked, rinsed
 and drained

1/2 cup sundried tomatoes, drained
1 red pepper, seeds and core removed,
 thinly sliced
2 cups baby rocket leaves

TOASTED PINE NUT DRESSING:

1/4 cup pine nuts, toasted
1 tblsp Dijon mustard
juice of 1 lemon

2 tblsp Colonna mandarin-infused olive oil
1/4 cup extra virgin olive oil
sea salt and freshly ground black pepper

1 Heat a large frying pan with a little oil and stir-fry prawns until just changed in colour. Remove to cool.

2 Place cold prawns, bocconcini, capers, sundried tomatoes, sliced red pepper and rocket into a salad bowl.

3 To prepare dressing, purée pine nuts, Dijon mustard and lemon juice in the bowl of a food processor. With the motor running, drizzle in oils to form a thick dressing. Season with salt and pepper to taste.

4 Pour dressing over salad and toss well to serve.

Recipe created by Julie Le Clerc

Wine: Te Koko

Writing about Te Koko in an overseas publication, wine writer, educator and Master of Wine, Bob Campbell paraphrased a line from Star Trek when he said, 'It's sauvignon blanc, Jim, but not as we know it.' That sums it up nicely. Not everybody likes this relatively new member of the Cloudy Bay portfolio, and that suits winemaker Kevin Judd and oenologist James Healy just fine. They never expected it to be an instant success – its layers of flavour are too complex for that. In this recipe, Julie has cleverly married those flavours with individual ingredients. Red pepper would work with either Cloudy Bay variant, but the toasted pine nuts echo Te Koko's gentle spicy oak, as does the touch of Dijon mustard.

It is sauvignon blanc that has put the Cloudy Bay label on the international wine map, but there are other strings to the company's bow. Chardonnay, pinot noir and a sparkling wine called Pelorus all enjoy a good reputation, and visitors to the cellar door might score a half-bottle of delicate riesling-based dessert wine if the vintage conditions have been kind. An even rarer high-alcohol gewürztraminer was a one-off a couple of years ago, but you never know, it might be repeated … one day. **VW**

Porcini & pinot noir risotto

SERVES 6

15g dried porcini

1/2 cup warm water

1 cup Mt Riley Pinot Noir

1 1/2 cups beef or chicken stock

2 tblsp olive oil

2 cloves garlic, crushed

1 onion, peeled and finely diced

2 stalks celery, finely diced

1 1/2 cups risotto rice (such as Italian
 Ferron brand, Vialone Nano or Carnaroli)

1/2 cup freshly grated Parmesan

2 tblsp chopped fresh mint

sea salt and freshly ground black pepper

1 Place porcini in warm water and leave to soak for 20 minutes. Squeeze porcini, slice and set aside. Filter soaking liquid through a sieve lined with a paper towel.

2 Heat porcini water, pinot noir and stock together in a saucepan.

3 Heat a large heavy-based pan, add oil, garlic, onion and celery and cook gently for 5 minutes. Add rice and stir for 2 minutes to toast but not brown. Add one ladleful of hot stock mixture and stir well. When the rice has absorbed the liquid, add another ladleful. Continue to stir and keep adding hot liquid until it is all absorbed. After 15–20 minutes the rice should be al dente and creamy. Stir in chopped porcini, Parmesan, mint, and salt and pepper to taste. Cover and leave to steam for 5 minutes.

4 Perfect served with barbecued Cervena/venison French rack.

Recipe created by Julie Le Clerc

Wine: Seventeen Valley Pinot Noir

Here is another example of a good match made even better by using a bit of the accompanying wine in the dish – although it already had a lot going for it. Pinot noir's soft, plummy flavours are perfect with game like hare, ostrich or Cervena, and the Seventeen Valley version also has a suggestion of mushrooms that ties in perfectly with the dried porcini.

Seventeen Valley wines come from a single site that is one of four owned by the company. A full-flavoured chardonnay was first out of the starting blocks, and it received instant fame when it topped its class in a major international competition. This pinot has been equally well received. Wines from the other Mount Riley vineyards include a nicely balanced sauvignon blanc, a stylish riesling, usually made close to bone-dry, and a blend of cabernet sauvignon and merlot. Most unusual wine in the portfolio is Savée, a sparkling sauvignon blanc. **VW**

Mount Riley

Our visit to Mount Riley begins with a pleasant drive on a hot summer's day. Sun-baked hills of desiccated grass and fractured lines of wind-blown dryness demonstrate how easy it must have been for a recent fire to take hold. The extent of the disaster manifests itself in acres of devastation. And yet a miracle vineyard at Seventeen Valley survived.

Seventeen Valley has a unique climate that is fantastic for grape growing. The vineyard consists of a series of terraces lying in a rain shadow, in this warm, sheltered valley. Here a weather station is conveniently located in the vineyard so that 'Digger' the winemaker can study the weather patterns. Every year the vintage is different, so he finds it useful to build up a wealth of data on the climatic history of the valley. Seventeen Valley is certainly a unique and special place, and gives its name to the top quality single vineyard Mount Riley wines. **JLeC**

Wairau River Wines

The simplicity and honesty of Wairau River's building suggests functionalism, which in no way ignores style. The strong lines of the rammed earth construction are striking. Being made of mud-bricks means this building is very much 'of the earth'. The space houses Wairau River's retail cellar door and popular restaurant. A cosy, heavy-beamed dining room spills out onto sun-drenched verandas, where the clink of glasses is as bright as the sounds of laughter coming from cheerful groups luxuriating under a grape arbour on the lawn.

Here, with a concise yet innovative menu, a local harvest of fresh food is imaginatively cooked and served in a classic vineyard setting. Partner food prepared on the premises with Wairau River's own delicious wines – they are awash with the fresh, penetrating flavours of Marlborough grapes. **JLeC**

Pizza of chorizo, feta & rocket pesto

SERVES 6

PIZZA BASE:

1/2 cup warm water	2 cups plain flour
1 tsp sugar	1/2 tsp sea salt
2 tsp active dried yeast	2 tblsp olive oil

1 Place warm water into a small bowl, sprinkle with sugar and then yeast. Leave to activate for 5–10 minutes until frothy.

2 Place flour and salt into a large bowl, make a well in the centre. Pour in oil and activated yeast mixture. Mix together into a firm dough, adding a little more water if necessary. Knead for 5 minutes. Place dough into a lightly oiled bowl and cover with plastic wrap. Leave to rise in a warm place until doubled in volume, this takes about 30–40 minutes.

3 Knock back dough by pressing firmly with fist and lightly knead again. Divide dough into 6 and roll each portion out thinly and place onto a lightly oiled baking tray.

4 Pre-heat oven to 200°C. Cover with a choice of topping ingredients. Bake for 20 minutes or until crust is golden and firm.

PIZZA TOPPING:

fresh tomato sauce

roasted vegetables

chorizo or spicy sausage

rocket or basil pesto (or use recipe on page 165)

olives

fresh basil

Recipe created by Chris Rose, Wairau River

Wine: Wairau River Sauvignon Blanc

Marlborough sauvignon blanc is right at home with salty cheese, and it loves herbs and vegetables. That makes this pizza, topped with cubes of feta, roasted vegetables, pesto, rocket and fresh basil a perfect match. Even the olives play a part in linking the plate and the glass.

Phil and Chris Rose once sold all their crop to other companies, but now they have a big reputation with their own label. Sauvignon blanc is the best-known member of the range, but a charming riesling, an understated chardonnay and, when weather permits, an excellent dessert wine are all available from the cellar shop and around the country. **VW**

Timara Lodge

Tumara Lodge

GROVE MILL WINERY

Wairau River Wines

Rhubarb & ginger syllabub with crisp ginger biscuits

SERVES 8

SYLLABUB:

500g rhubarb, cut into small chunks

1/4 cup sugar

2 cups cream

1/2 cup ginger wine (to taste)

8 pieces ginger preserved in syrup, drained and slivered

1 Place rhubarb and sugar into a saucepan, cover and cook over a gentle heat for about 30 minutes until soft. Purée mixture in a blender and leave to cool.

2 Whip cream and ginger wine together. Stir in slivered ginger and rhubarb purée.

3 Divide mixture between serving glasses. Chill to serve and decorate with extra ginger if desired. Serve with crisp ginger biscuits.

CRISP GINGER BISCUITS: MAKES 24

175g chilled butter, cut into cubes

175g caster sugar

175g self-raising flour

2 heaped tsp ground ginger

1 Pre-heat oven to 130°C. Line a baking tray with non-stick baking paper.

2 Place all ingredients into the bowl of a food processor and process until mixture forms a ball.

3 Take walnut-sized pieces of dough and slightly flatten onto prepared tray.

4 Bake for 1 1/2 hours (to create similar texture to meringues) until light and crisp. Remove to a wire rack to cool. Store in an airtight container.

Recipe created by chef Jeremy Jones, Timara Lodge

WINE: SPY VALLEY GEWÜRZTRAMINER

Gewürztraminer is a distinctive variety that often has a strong suggestion of fresh ginger in its bouquet. That makes it a perfect match for Jeremy's ginger biscuits on their own. Add the syllabub, which contains both ginger wine and ginger syrup, and you can't go wrong! The final link in the chain is the rhubarb. Its sweet/sour flavour is echoed by the sweet start but faintly bitter finish of the wine.

Spy Valley may be a new company, but it is already showing a lot of promise. First wines, sauvignon blanc, chardonnay, pinot noir and merlot, were all made by leasing equipment in another company's plant, but plans are afoot to build a winery by the third vintage. **VW**

SPY VALLEY WINES & TIMARA LODGE

The vineyards of Johnson Estate have been growing grapes to supply a large winery for some time now, and have only recently begun producing their own wines under the Spy Valley Wines label. The name comes from the Waihopai Valley, christened 'spy valley' due to the presence of large spherical communication satellites. More wines are due to come on stream, and a winery is planned on site.

Linked to the same company is the sophisticated retreat, Timara Lodge. Boutique accommodation and a luxury food and wine experience are provided, complete with a lakeside garden setting, elegant formal gardens and lap pool secluded by a perfectly manicured hedge. Guest menus vary from day to day and are crafted to emphasise Marlborough produce and wines. The kitchen seeks out individual growers throughout the region to gain produce picked that morning for the foundation ingredients of every dish. The whole encounter is delicious. **JLeC**

Grove Mill

Grove Mill abides well in the glorious landscape of Marlborough. The company's founding mission statement is to be 'style makers, not style followers'. With integrity, Grove Mill pioneered natural, sensitive vineyard management techniques to enhance the regional character of their wines, and to sustain and develop the Grove Mill style. This style is for full-flavoured wines, each with its own distinctive personality and the definitive taste of Marlborough in each and every glass. Winemaker David Pearce says evocatively of Grove Mill Riesling, 'It is particularly nice to drink in the afternoon under a tree.'

Grove Mill takes an educative role, and offers wine-learning experiences such as a vine library, blind tastings by arrangement or aroma demonstrations, which help identify facets of their wines. The dramatic tasting room is also a gallery space, the walls awash with quirky and colourful exhibitions by leading contemporary New Zealand artists. **JLeC**

Apricot & ginger tarte tatin

MAKES 1 TART TO SERVE 8

125g butter, cubed and chilled	1 1/2 cups plain flour
1 tblsp grated fresh ginger	2 tblsp sugar
finely grated zest of 1 lime	2–3 tblsp ice-cold water

CARAMELISED APRICOTS:

25g butter	1/2 cup sugar
1 tsp orange flower water (optional if unobtainable)	10 fresh apricots, halved (or 825g can apricot halves, drained and dried
1 tblsp water	on a paper towel)

1 Rub butter, ginger and lime zest into flour and sugar until crumbly. Add water and combine into a firm dough. Chill for 20 minutes. Roll out pastry on a lightly floured board to form a circle 25cm in diameter, 5mm thick. Prick with a fork and rest until required.
2 Pre-heat oven to 200°C. Melt butter in a 24cm frying pan with an ovenproof handle. Add orange flower water, water and sugar. Shake over heat until lightly caramelised, this takes about 5 minutes.
3 Remove from heat, arrange apricot halves, skin side down in caramel in the frying pan. Cover apricots with pastry circle, the loose fit is to allow for shrinkage during cooking. Bake for 30 minutes.
4 Remove from oven, allow to cool and firm up in pan for 5 minutes before turning out so that fruit is on the surface. Serve while still warm.

Recipe created by Julie Le Clerc

Wine: Grove Mill Riesling

David Pearce likes to leave enough natural sweetness in his rieslings to lift the fruit and add weight, but they always manage to retain lively acids. A full-on dessert wine would be too much for this savoury dessert, but the medium-sweet Grove Mill Riesling is perfect with it. The lime and orange blossom flavours match the same characters in the wine, and the ginger ties in with the spicy finish.

Dave Pearce has been with Grove Mill since the days when his tanks, presses and other winemaking paraphernalia were crammed into a former granary right in the middle of Blenheim. He has produced some excellent wines over the years, many of which have won awards. The range includes sauvignon blanc, pinot gris, riesling, chardonnay, pinot noir, merlot and – unusually – pinotage, made from a grape that is grown only in New Zealand and South Africa. **VW**

AS THE TITLE OF THIS CHAPTER SUGGESTS,

CANTERBURY/
WAIPARA
ARE TWO
REGIONS
WITHIN ONE.

Mountford Vineya

THE FIRST LATTER-DAY WINEMAKERS planted grapes on the plains south of Christchurch. It wasn't easy. Cruelly cold winds made it difficult to ripen the crops, and constant vigilance was needed to prevent frost damage. But these pioneers persisted, and some very good wines were produced once the vines reached maturity. The Giesens, who run one of Canterbury's few large properties, summed up the local attitude when they said they chose their site because their German heritage had taught them to grow grapes where there was real change with the seasons.

In recent years, most of the growth in Canterbury has been occurring north of Christchurch, in the Waipara Valley.

Frost can still be a problem, but shelter from the Teviotdale Hills means the valley is less troubled by freezing winds. Like many of the country's grape-growing regions, the local soil is mostly gravelly and free-draining, a legacy of the time when it was criss-crossed with meandering rivers.

A trip that takes in the areas north and south of Christchurch is a rewarding one. Cantabrians are commendably loyal, and the many restaurants and cafés that have sprung up on the wine trail offer local wines accompanied by food prepared from ingredients often raised or grown within sight of the vines.

Both sub-regions produce particularly exciting wines from the riesling grape, but other varieties also perform well. Chardonnay, pinot gris and, in the red corner, pinot noir are all capable of producing excellent wines in the best vintages, and a couple of top awards have been won for sauvignon blanc. The local climate would seem to be tailor-made for sparkling wine, but surprisingly few examples have been produced.

Canterbury/Waipara doesn't have the same high profile as other regions, but it has a great heritage and an exciting future. VW

SALT & SPICE-ROASTED DUCK WITH TRUFFLE MASH

SERVES 4

4 single boneless duck breasts, trimmed

2 tblsp grated fresh ginger

1 tsp ground cardamom

1 tsp ground cinnamon

1 tsp ground fennel seeds

1/4 tsp chilli powder

1 tsp Maldon sea salt flakes

1 With a sharp knife, score the skin of each duck breast to help release fat during cooking. Place duck breasts into a non-metallic dish. Mix spices together and rub firmly all over duck breasts. Leave to marinate for 3–4 hours.

2 Heat a frying pan with an ovenproof handle over medium heat and place duck breasts skin side down to cook for 2 minutes. Pour off duck fat then cook for 2 more minutes. Pour off fat, turn breasts over and place in oven preheated to 180°C for 5 minutes or until the juices run slightly pink and meat is medium rare.

3 Serve sprinkled with Maldon salt and truffle oil-drizzled mash.

TRUFFLE MASH:

600g floury potatoes

50g butter, melted

1/4–1/2 cup hot milk

2 tblsp truffle-infused oil (or more to taste)

1 Boil potatoes until tender, drain and briefly return to heat to evaporate any remaining moisture. Mash well. Beat in butter and milk until smooth and creamy. Lastly whip in truffle oil.

Recipe created by Julie Le Clerc

WINE: KAITUNA VALLEY PINOT NOIR

When the 1998 version of this wine topped its class at a major *Cuisine* magazine tasting, enthusiasts all over the country scrambled for their maps. Kaituna Valley has been making wine since the 1993 vintage, but it has never had a high profile. Partly, that's because pinot was the only variety produced until a newly purchased sauvignon blanc site in Marlborough came on stream.

Duck and pinot is a classic combination, so it seemed a logical choice for a dish to match with wine from a specialist in the variety. Extra flavour links are provided by the truffle oil, which ties in with pinot's celebrated earthiness, and the cardamom, which reflects the smoky notes of the charred oak barrels in which the wine was aged. **VW**

KAITUNA VALLEY

Surrounded by protective hills on three of four sides lies Kaituna Valley, a small family-owned estate producing wines of the highest quality – like their bold and dramatically complex pinot noir, which has a wonderful spread of flavours. Abundant soft textual tannins balance masses of black cherry and powerful plum flavours, along with a suggestion of exotic spice backed by the underlying smokiness of toasty oak.

This very individual wine is crafted from the hand-harvested grapes of low-yielding vineyards in the Kaituna Valley, Banks Peninsula, which is on the way from Christchurch to Akaroa. This young winery is setting new standards, and owner/winemaker Grant Whelen has good reason to consider Kaituna Valley to be 'at the forefront of the next generation of pinot noir producers'. **JLeC**

Giesen Wine estate

Giesen Wine Estate is situated on the picturesque Canterbury Plains, south of the city of Christchurch. This area experiences a cooler climate due to its proximity to the Southern Alps. The cool climate enables the fruit to ripen slowly and develop complex fruit flavours as well as good levels of acidity – a backbone for longevity in wines. These elegantly crafted wines show a distinct 'vintage character'.

This export-orientated winery is very much a family affair, being owned and managed by three brothers. A nice personalised touch is the tradition of reproducing paintings on the labels by New Zealand artists, which express the character of each wine. **JLeC**

Hot-smoked salmon hash cakes

SERVES 4

600g floury potatoes
2 tblsp butter, melted
400g hot-smoked salmon, flaked (available in supermarkets)
1 small red onion, very finely chopped
1/4 cup salted capers, rinsed and chopped
2 tblsp chopped fresh coriander
sea salt and freshly ground black pepper
1 egg, beaten
1 tbsp milk
2 cups dry breadcrumbs
lime or lemon wedges to serve

1 Cook potatoes in boiling salted water until tender. Drain well and mash with butter. Cool.
2 Add flaked salmon to potato with onion, capers, coriander and salt and pepper to taste. Form mixture into eight thick patties.
3 Beat egg and milk together and spread breadcrumbs out on a tray. Dip patties in egg and then crumbs to coat.
4 Heat a frypan with a little olive oil and gently fry fishcakes until golden brown on both sides.
5 Serve with lime or lemon wedges on the side.

Recipe created by Julie Le Clerc

Wine: Giesen Canterbury Reserve Chardonnay

Hot-smoked salmon might suggest sauvignon blanc, but look at the other ingredients in this gutsy dish. The texture of the potatoes ties in nicely with the smoothness of the 1998 Reserve Chardonnay, a legacy of an acid-softening malolactic fermentation. Toasty oak is echoed by the breadcrumb coating, and the smoky character of the fish itself enhances the effect. A gentle squeeze of lemon or lime juice will link in with chardonnay's citric notes.

Alex, Theo and Marcel Giesen have big plans for the future, and have recently been on a land-buying spree in Marlborough. But their hearts are in Canterbury, where they have carved out a solid reputation. They are probably best known for a series of impeccably balanced rieslings, but it is their chardonnays that have won more awards. A recent trophy for top sauvignon blanc at a major US wine show raised their export sales considerably, and they have also made top-class pinot noir, as well as some of the sexiest dessert wines in the country. All in all, an impressive act! **VW**

St Helena Wine Estate

St Helena Wine Estate is perched just north of the city of Christchurch among the rich tapestry of New Zealand's Canterbury Plains. The vineyard takes full advantage of the area's ideal climate, producing excellent grapes in good years.

St Helena holds the distinction of producing a landmark wine – the company is acknowledged as the pioneer of pinot noir in New Zealand. The vines are some of the oldest in the country, giving St Helena some of the advantages of Burgundy, most notably the age of the vines and the full ripeness of the variety.

The St Helena pinot is medium-bodied with soft tannins. A dessert pairing may seem unexpected, but in fact makes a great combination. As the pinot noir is of a lighter style than some, it is well suited to the berry flavours of summer. The brioche is in turn very complementary to the toastiness of oak in the wine. **JLeC**

TOASTED BRIOCHE WITH SUMMER PUDDING FRUITS

SERVES 6

1 cup strawberries
1 cup raspberries
1 cup red currants or blueberries
1/4 cup St Helena Pinot Noir
1/2 cup sugar
6 slices brioche

1   Hull strawberries and slice in half. Pick over raspberries and remove stems from red currants. Place into a saucepan with pinot noir and sugar. Bring to the boil then gently simmer for 5–10 minutes or until reduced and syrupy. Be careful not to break up fruit. Remove to a bowl and chill for a few hours or preferably overnight.
2   Next day, just before serving, toast brioche and top with summer pudding fruits.

Recipe created by Julie Le Clerc

WINE: ST HELENA PINOT NOIR

The first St Helena Pinot Noir came from the 1982 vintage, and it won a gold medal. Winemaker Danny Schuster, now in charge of his own Omihi Hills vineyard, repeated the exercise in 1984, inspiring many local growers to plant this temperamental variety. It was a prophetic move – pinot noir is now being touted as New Zealand's great red hope for the future. The 1999 version tested alongside this berry-based dessert has pleasant raspberry and cherry characters that link nicely with the fruit. It's an unusual combination, but it works well.

St Helena has gained in strength and reputation in recent times. Two tiers of wine are produced, with the top bottles carrying 'reserve' status. Most unusual is a simple but attractive pinot blanc, but the collection also includes pinot gris, chardonnay and sauvignon blanc. The Reserve Chardonnay, particularly, is well worth searching out. **VW**

Pegasus Bay

Fiddlers Green

Waipara West

Waipara West is a family-based business situated a little off the beaten track, near the gorge of the Waipara River. It takes its name from a weather station situated on the property. A barn-like winery building, the colour of tussock grass, now blends beautifully with the land around it. Amazingly, after the land was purchased by the partnership it was discovered that members of the same family had previously owned the farm at the turn of the century.

Waipara has many natural advantages that have created a near-perfect environment for high quality wine production. The sheltered vineyards of Waipara West sit in a hot basin collecting warmth from the region's long, hot dry summers. Vines are planted on naturally sloping shingle terraces, which vary in height and aspect but are totally invisible from the road. The philosophy of Waipara West is to craft wines to reflect this spectacularly unique environment and the natural quality of the fruit. **JLeC**

Anchovy & olive lamb with beetroot orzo

SERVES 4

1 cup orzo (a rice-shaped pasta)
2 beetroot, cooked, peeled and sliced
1 tblsp whole grain mustard
1 clove garlic, crushed
2 tblsp extra virgin olive oil
4 lamb shortloins (backstraps), trimmed
12 anchovy fillets (fleshy Ortiz anchovies are the best you'll ever taste)
12 pitted black olives (I adore pitted Salvagno olives from Verona)
1 tblsp butter, softened
sea salt and freshly ground black pepper
fresh mint leaves

1 Cook orzo in boiling salted water for 8–10 minutes or until just tender. Drain and toss with hot sliced beetroot, mustard, garlic and olive oil, seasoning with salt and pepper to taste.
2 With a small sharp knife, make incisions into the lamb flesh. Insert into these a sliver of olive and a piece of anchovy, pushing them deep into the meat. Cream remaining anchovies with butter and smear over the meat. Season with freshly ground black pepper.
3 Heat a pan, cook lamb for 3 minutes on each side for medium rare. Remove to rest for 10 minutes before slicing.
4 Serve lamb sliced on top of beetroot orzo with mint to garnish.

Recipe created by Julie Le Clerc

Wine: Waipara West Ram Paddock Red

This likeable blend of cabernet franc, cabernet sauvignon and merlot makes a good partner for lamb, and the addition of olives and anchovies certainly does the match no harm. The wine has a faintly herbal edge that links to the saltiness in both ingredients, and makes it rather more enjoyable with food than it is on its own – which is very much part of the Waipara West philosophy.

Waipara West enjoys a big reputation for its smoky, sweet-fruited pinot noir, but it is often hard to find. A lively sauvignon blanc and a well-focused chardonnay are both popular with the fans, but neither is made in big quantities. **VW**

CANTERBURY HOUSE WINERY

Canterbury House is a relatively new estate vineyard and winery in Waipara, North Canterbury. The enterprise was sparked off during a New Zealand vacation by a couple from California who toured and fell in love with the country and its people. This encounter, combined with a long-term interest in wine, turned into a vineyard in New Zealand. Future expansion of both the vineyard and visitor facility is planned to continue in a 'measured fashion'.

Surrounded by vines and a lovely enclosed courtyard, the restaurant is large-scale but retains a warm ambience. The varied menu highlights the delights of New Zealand produce by featuring dishes such as an intriguing peppered North Canterbury ostrich salad. **JLeC**

SALAD OF BABY BEETROOT & FETA WITH SALSA ROSSO

SERVES 4

SALSA ROSSO:

2 red peppers, roasted until blistering then put in a plastic bag to sweat until skins are easily removed

2 tblsp olive oil

1 clove garlic, crushed

1 fresh red chilli, seeded and finely chopped

1 tblsp fresh marjoram

4 ripe tomatoes, chopped

sea salt and freshly ground black pepper

1　Peel and seed the peppers, then chop flesh finely. Heat the oil in a heavy-based saucepan and fry garlic gently. Add chilli, marjoram and tomatoes and cook for 30 minutes or until tomatoes are reduced. Add the peppers and cook a further 5 minutes. Season with salt and pepper to taste.

SALAD:

200g whole baby beetroot, cooked, peeled and halved

50g snow peas, blanched

3 tblsp pine nuts, toasted

100g feta cheese, cubed

2 cups dressed salad leaves

1　To assemble the salad place dressed salad leaves in a bowl. Top with beetroot, snow peas, pine nuts and feta. Serve with salsa rosso and grilled polenta as shown in photograph (optional).

Recipe created by chef Trudi Jones, Canterbury House

WINE: CANTERBURY HOUSE PINOT GRIS

The flavours in this salad make several wines a possibility. The capsicum and feta cheese suggest sauvignon blanc, the pine nuts are often partnered with chardonnay and the beetroot could find associations with riesling or even pinot noir. In the end, the kitchen team gave the nod to pinot gris because of its versatility. It has a graininess that brings out the best in the grilled polenta, and a suggestion of sweetness that matches the beetroot and counteracts the saltiness of the feta. Marjoram provides the final link.

Canterbury House aims to gain an international reputation for top quality pinot noir, and early examples certainly show promise. In the meantime, most competition success has been achieved with sauvignon blanc, but good wine has also been made from riesling, merlot and chardonnay. A méthode traditionnelle sparkler has a keen following around the Canterbury region. **VW**

ROCKET & LEMON PESTO

MAKES ABOUT 1 1/2 CUPS

4 cloves garlic, peeled

1 cup rocket leaves, tightly packed

1/2 cup parsley leaves, tightly packed

finely grated rind and juice of one lemon

1 tsp sea salt

1/4 cup pine nuts

1/4 cup grated Parmesan

1/4 cup extra virgin olive oil

1   Place garlic, rocket and parsley leaves, lemon rind and juice into the bowl of a food processor and pulse well to chop.
2   Add salt, pine nuts and Parmesan and process until well blended. With motor running drizzle in oil to form a smooth paste.
3   Use to spread on crostini, as a dip for vegetables and bread, or as a sauce for pasta or pizza.

Recipe created by Julie Le Clerc

WINE: FIDDLER'S GREEN SAUVIGNON BLANC

Rocket, parsley, garlic and lemon rind? That's tailor-made sauvignon blanc territory, and the Fiddler's Green reading of the style has just the right sort of vivacity to make it work.

Fiddler's Green produces only a handful of styles. The sauvignon is joined by an attractive riesling, usually made on the sweet side of medium, and a sparkling wine is also in the pipeline. High hopes are held for a gently fruited pinot noir that has recently joined the portfolio.

The winery name is no flight of fancy? Well, not a contemporary one. Apparently a nautical type named the property now occupied by this tiny vineyard because he saw it as 'a happy land where there is perpetual mirth, and a fiddle that never stops playing for sailors who never tire'. **VW**

FIDDLER'S GREEN

Fiddler's Green is a relative newcomer to the Waipara winery scene, but is already making quite an impression. Mighty double gates announce the entrance to the estate, and once inside a lush environment welcomes visitors. Anticipation builds with the journey down the driveway lined with vines and olive trees to the Mediterranean-inspired building. Residing in the attractive rural landscape among the grapevines, this charming building houses the tasting room and sales cellar.

Producing handcrafted wines solely from grapes grown on this estate, Fiddler's Green's owners have set their mission towards developing a wine style that reflects the uniqueness of the site. With this goal in mind they present wines of high quality, style and elegance. **JLeC**

ROASTED SALMON WITH SWEET DILL CUCUMBER & LIME SOUR CREAM

SERVES 4

800g fresh salmon fillet, skin on, fine pin bones removed

1/2 telegraph cucumber, peeled, halved and seeds removed

1 tblsp olive oil

1/4 cup Pegasus Bay Sauvignon Blanc Sémillon

2 tblsp chopped fresh dill

sea salt and freshly ground black pepper

1/4 cup sour cream

juice of 1 lime

1   Cut salmon fillet into 4 portions. Heat a heavy pan, add a little oil and seal salmon, then place in the oven at 200°C for 8 minutes.
2   Slice cucumber halves and toss into a hot saucepan with olive oil. Add wine, dill, salt and pepper and toss well.
3   Blend sour cream and lime juice together.
4   Serve salmon on top of cucumber with a dollop of lime sour cream. Garnish with fresh dill or chevril.

Adapted from a recipe by chef Tim Knight, Pegasus Bay

WINE: PEGASUS BAY SAUVIGNON BLANC/SÉMILLON

They're keen food lovers at Pegasus Bay, and this is a very good match. Just look at the ingredients – salmon, cucumber, dill and lime juice, all tailor-made to match the edgy, upfront characters of the two varieties in the blend. Even the strident notes of sour cream add to the mix. Great stuff!

The Donaldsons have done more than anybody to raise the profile of Waipara around New Zealand and the world. Their wines often stray way off the established flavour trails, but there are very few duds. Chardonnay, pinot noir and especially riesling have been used to craft some splendid wines over the years. Even Bordeaux varieties like cabernet sauvignon and merlot – not, on the face of it, ideal grapes for the local climate – have been coaxed to perform above expectations in good years. This is very much a name to watch. A second wine portfolio, labelled Main Divide, often includes grapes from outside the area, and offers some very good buys. **VW**

PEGASUS BAY

Diners at Pegasus Bay can promenade in the striking park-like gardens before enjoying a sensational wine and food experience. They can relax afterwards in a private part of the garden to watch late summer shadows fall across pieces gathered from a sculpture symposium. There is also the lake to be explored, winding pathways dotted with arbours and other hidden nooks and crannies. This magical setting is home not only to a top quality winery but also a stunning restaurant, where food and wine are skilfully paired.

Excellent but unpretentious food is chosen from an innovative menu that incorporates very helpful wine suggestions. With this vibrant example, the winemakers say they aimed to make a food-friendly wine. They felt that sauvignon blanc was 'a bit one dimensional', so sémillon was added 'to produce a more complete and complex wine'. **JLeC**

Muddy Water Fine Wines

It is easy to miss the driveway up to Muddy Water's winery but this special place is certainly worth finding. Swallows circle low over vines, sunny fields of flowers and an elevated dam created for irrigation. The winery buildings are extraordinary – made of straw bales, cement-plastered on both sides and painted the colour of soft earth. The whole facility feels very much a part of the district; in fact, the bales of straw came from a farm up the road. This type of construction also provides excellent and natural insulation. Another form of natural temperature control exists in the barrel room, where an air exchange method is employed using fans and vents to maintain a constant temperature for the wine.

Muddy Water (the translation of Waipara) is positioned on the gentle slopes of the Waipara Valley, a region chosen because it experiences a special meso-climate favouring the production of intensely flavoured grapes. These premium grapes are all estate grown, yielding handmade wines that are 'literally made in the field'. **JLeC**

Mediterranean lamb burgers with beetroot & pinot noir relish

SERVES 4

BEETROOT PINOT NOIR RELISH:

2 tblsp olive oil	1 large beetroot, peeled and grated
1 medium red onion, finely sliced	1/2 tsp black pepper
3 tblsp finely grated fresh ginger	1/2 cup sugar
1 red chilli, seeds removed and	1/2 cup red wine vinegar
finely chopped	1 cup Muddy Water Pinot Noir

1 Heat a large saucepan, add oil and cook onion to soften. Add remaining ingredients, bring to the boil then simmer for 20–30 minutes until well reduced and syrupy. Store in the refrigerator.

LAMB BURGERS:

500g lamb mince	1 tblsp each chopped fresh mint and parsley
1 egg, beaten	1 tsp ground cinnamon
1 red onion, minced or grated	finely grated zest of 1 lemon
3 cloves garlic, crushed	1/2 cup black olives, pitted and chopped

1 Mix all ingredients together with your hands, squeezing to blend well. Divide mixture into 8 patties.
2 Heat a pan, add a little oil and cook burgers over medium heat for 3–4 minutes on each side. Drain on paper towels.
3 Serve two burgers per person topped with relish.

Recipe created by Julie Le Clerc

Wine: Muddy Water Pinot Noir

The slogan 'Drink Muddy Water' certainly got people talking when the owners of this new property dreamed it up. It wouldn't have worked if the product wasn't up to it, but the quality of the wines was excellent right from the first vintage. The pinot matches this dish because it has a wealth of ripe fruit characters to bring out the best in the lamb, to link with the beetroot in the relish and to emphasise the sweetness of the red onion.

Chardonnay, riesling and a fruit salad of a red called Laborare, a blend of cabernet sauvignon, cabernet franc, merlot, shiraz, sangiovese and pinotage, are included in the Muddy Water range. The standard is uniformly high, but the wines are often hard to find because many cases head off overseas. **VW**

Mountford Vineyard

Muddy Water Fine Wines

Mountford Vineyard

Muddy Water Fine Wines

Mountford Vineyard

Mountford is an extremely pretty hillside vineyard dedicated to producing top quality pinot noir and chardonnay. Charming accommodation, two rooms with a view, is included in the attractive homestead, providing visitors with an unforgettable lifestyle vineyard stay. Guests have access to all the delights of the region, plus the exceptionally good cooking and hospitality of hosts Buffy and Michael Eaton. The featured recipe was developed from a suggestion by Buffy, who says white peaches are imperative.

Note: Vincotto is a new discovery in this part of the world, but it has been produced by the Calogiuri family in Italy since 1825. Prepared from a carefully guarded secret recipe, it is made by cooking the must of late-harvested grapes over a low flame. This mixture is then aged with a mother must in oak casks. Not overly sweet, vincotto is a delectable syrupy condiment. **JLeC**

Roasted white peaches with prosciutto, Parmesan & vincotto

SERVES 4

4 white peaches
1–2 tblsp extra virgin olive oil
50g thinly sliced prosciutto
50g shaved fresh Parmesan
3–4 tblsp vincotto (see note opposite)

1 Halve peaches and remove stones. Rub peach halves lightly with olive oil and place cut side up onto an oven tray. Roast in oven preheated to 200°C for 25–30 minutes until soft and caramelised. Remove to cool.

2 Serve roast peaches drizzled with vincotto and draped with prosciutto and Parmesan shavings.

Recipe created by Julie Le Clerc, inspired by Buffy Eaton

Wine: Mountford Chardonnay

Chardonnay is often described as peachy, so it was a natural choice for this highly original sweet and savoury dish. Julie sometimes uses a light dusting of icing sugar to form a glaze on the fruit, and although it makes the dish slightly sweeter, it doesn't throw the balance out thanks to the earthy graininess of the Parmesan. And the vincotto? That makes the whole thing more interesting!

Mountford wines are hard to find away from the winery and homestead, but they are well worth searching for. So far, this big-hearted chardonnay and a nicely tuned pinot noir make up the entire range, but pinot gris and gewürztraminer are both performing well in the vineyard – watch this space! **VW**

A charming courtyard surrounded by attractive old buildings greets visitors to Waipara Springs Wines. The buildings have quite a past – the winery and restaurant were converted from historic stables, a farm wool shed and an implement shed.

The restaurant is open all year round and offers a great café-style menu. The kitchen strives to feature as many local ingredients as possible in their dishes, including farmhouse-style cheeses, lamb, salmon and seasonal local fruit and vegetables. Famous, freshly baked bread is made on the premises. A particularly nice touch is the ever-changing 'meal of the day', and this is where options such as the featured tart might appear. Wining and dining alfresco under the shade of colourful umbrellas in the pretty courtyard setting is a wonderful experience. **JLeC**

ROASTED RED PEPPER, POTATO & HIPI ITI TART

SERVES 8

300g savoury short crust pastry

5 red peppers

2–3 medium waxy potatoes, peeled and cooked

1/2 cup sour cream

1/2 cup cream

1 tblsp whole grain mustard

1 whole egg plus 3 egg yolks

sea salt and freshly ground black pepper

100g Hipi iti (NZ sheep's feta or other feta cheese)

1 Pre-heat oven to 200°C. Roll out pastry to 3mm thick and use to line a 24cm loose-based, fluted tart tin. Prick with a fork, cover with non-stick baking paper or foil and fill with baking beans. Bake blind for 10–15 minutes. Remove paper and beans and return to oven for 5 minutes more.

2 Place whole peppers onto an oven tray and roast at 200°C for 30–40 minutes until blackened and blistering. Remove and put in a plastic bag to sweat. Once cool enough to handle the skins will peel away easily. Discard skin, seeds and stalk. Line pastry case with peppers then cover with a layer of sliced potato.

3 Blend sour cream, cream, mustard, egg and yolks together and season with salt and pepper to taste. Pour over peppers and potato and top with slices of feta.

4 Bake at 200°C for 20–25 minutes until mixture has just set and is golden brown.

5 Serve warm with salad.

Recipe created by Rex MacKenzie, Waipara Springs Winery Restaurant

WINE: WAIPARA SPRINGS CHARDONNAY

Waipara Springs makes both sauvignon blanc and chardonnay, and either wine would make a good match for this dish. The peppers and Hipi iti cheese would tie in nicely with the sauvignon, but the potatoes and cream change the texture, making chardonnay a logical choice.

Other wines in the range include a pleasantly citric riesling and a middleweight pinot noir. Cabernet sauvignon, not a common variety in the South Island but seen more often in Waipara than elsewhere, is popular at the cellar door, but suffers from greenness in all but the hottest years. **VW**

IF YOU ENJOY A TOUCH OF
DRAMA WITH YOUR GLASS OF WINE,
CENTRAL
OTAGO
IS THE PLACE TO BE.

Rippon Vineyard

Gibbston Valley Wines

Chard Farm

THE RUGGED LANDSCAPE seems to bring out the pioneer spirit in grape growers and winemakers, and vineyards have been established in some pretty perilous locations as a result.

From small beginnings in the 1990s, Central Otago is now New Zealand's fourth largest winemaking region, and in most years it is the fastest growing. We think of it as being cold, and certainly frost is a major problem. But every summer, the area also boasts some of the hottest temperatures in the country, often in excess of 30 degrees.

The sunny day, cool night weather pattern is ideal for riesling, pinot gris and pinot noir, but many excellent chardonnays have also been produced by local winemakers.

The first vineyards to make a nationwide name for themselves were Gibbston Valley and Chard Farm, both near Queenstown, and Rippon, a couple of hours away on the shores of Lake Wanaka. Later plantings have centred on the Bannockburn region, where the grapes mostly ripen a week or two earlier than their cityside cousins.

Growing grapes and making wine in Central Otago will always be a challenge – the widely varying temperatures will see to that. But some of the world's most interesting wines come from places where conditions could never be described as moderate.

A faded newspaper clipping on the wall of the original Rippon Vineyards winery shed summed up the local attitude. 'The world's greatest wines are made by men who wear overcoats,' the headline reads. The article probably referred to Germany, but if we ignore its presumptuous sexism, it could well have been referring to Central Otago. **VW**

GIBBSTON VALLEY WINES

A dramatic cave tunnels into solid alpine schist forming a must-see highlight for visitors to Gibbston Valley Wines. Regular interactive tours take in the vineyard and working winery, and culminate with wine tasting in the arresting atmosphere of the wine cave. This is not a mere curiosity, but the perfect haven for maturing wines. Classical recitals and other events held during the year take full advantage of the cave's magnificent acoustics.

Definitely take the opportunity to lunch at Gibbston Valley. In the delightful courtyard, shelter from the midday sun under giant umbrellas and feast on stylish and tasty food. The inspirational menu incorporates an imaginative blending of techniques and ingredients, some locally grown and others that trace their origins from around the globe. Keen attention is given to matching individual dishes with wines produced on-site. **JLeC**

TUNA CROQUE WITH SUNDRIED TOMATO RELISH

SERVES 4

sheet of focaccia bread, cut into wedges
basil pesto (available from delicatessens)
char-grilled eggplant slices
600g fresh tuna cut into 4
sliced tomato
lemon wedges
black olives

1. Split 2 wedges of focaccia in half lengthways and toast. Spread with pesto and top with eggplant slices.
2. Heat a char-grill pan, season tuna and grill briefly, turning once to leave centre rare. Place tuna onto eggplant and top with a good spoonful of sundried tomato relish. Serve with tomato slices, lemon wedges and olives.

SUNDRIED TOMATO RELISH:

500g onions, peeled and finely sliced
1/4 cup olive oil
125g chopped sundried tomatoes
juice of 2 lemons
2 tblsp lemon-infused olive oil
2 tblsp quality balsamic vinegar
sea salt and freshly ground black pepper

1. Place onions and olive oil into a saucepan and cook gently until softened and golden. Add remaining ingredients and cook on a medium/low heat until thick and reduced. Store in the refrigerator.

Recipe created by chef Mark Sage, Gibbston Valley Wines

WINE: GIBBSTON VALLEY SAUVIGNON BLANC

Pesto, eggplant, lemon, olives – this is tailor-made sauvignon territory. Most years, the Gibbston Valley version is intensely focused, and that provides plenty of flavour links with this upfront dish.

Gibbston Valley is one of the few Central Otago wineries large enough to have achieved a nationwide reputation with pretty well its entire range. Most success has been achieved with a series of nicely fruited rieslings, but good examples of chardonnay and pinot noir also have a keen following. **VW**

Classic oatcakes with Brie

MAKES 24

3 cups rolled oats
1 cup wholemeal flour
1/2 tsp salt
1/4 cup brown sugar, firmly packed
60g butter, cubed
1/4 cup golden syrup
1/4 cup plus 2 tblsp milk

1　Process 2 cups of the oats until finely ground and place into a large bowl with remaining oats, flour, salt and sugar. Rub butter into these dry ingredients until mixture resembles fine crumbs.
2　Warm golden syrup and milk together and pour onto dry ingredients. Mix together to form a soft, smooth dough.
3　Roll out dough to 3mm thick. If this is hard to do, try rolling between 2 sheets of baking paper. Cut into 7cm rounds with a pastry cutter. Place onto a greased baking tray. Prick with a fork and bake in an oven pre-heated to 180°C for 12 minutes or until golden brown. Remove to a rack to cool. Store in an airtight container.
4　Serve oat biscuits with soft cheese such as Whitestone Brie and quince paste.

Recipe created by Julie Le Clerc

WINE: FELTON ROAD RESERVE CHARDONNAY

Texture is at least as important as taste when matching wine and food, which is why the Felton Road team likes to accompany their creamy 2000-vintage chardonnay with a nice, oozy brie. Julie's oatcakes enhance the match by linking with the toasted nut notes of the oak barrels in which the wine was fermented and matured.

Few labels have made as much impact in a short time as Felton Road. Pinot noir and riesling, each made in two or three styles, were the first to grab the public's attention, achieving cult status within their first two vintages They deserved it. The two pinots are luxuriously fruited and gloriously smooth, and the rieslings boast impressive fruit intensity whether they are made dry, medium or sweet. Both oaked and unoaked chardonnays have been produced, and both have been very well received. **VW**

FELTON ROAD

Rows of lavender along the driveway greet visitors to the Felton Road estate. The vineyard is surrounded by a dramatic high-country landscape; beautiful light falls onto strong hills caressing the folds in the land. The Felton Road site is situated one gully west of the historic Bannockburn gold-fields, and was previously home to sheep and wild thyme. A unique three-level gravity flow winery is built into the hillside, integrating innovative modern ideas with the rustic simplicity typically found in Burgundian cellars and cuveries.

Every step possible is taken in the vineyard to guarantee that grapes of outstanding quality are delivered to the winery, as the quality of wine is essentially determined in the vineyard. Vines are meticulously managed by hand to ensure optimum quality fruit production. A philosophy of 'minimal winemaking intervention' is followed to allow the unique characters of the vineyard to be fully expressed. In this way, Felton Road wines are able to express complexity and personality rather than technicality. **JLeC**

Chard Farm

A courtesy warning is issued to Chard Farm visitors to watch the driveway. This advice can only be fully understood when the journey is undertaken along the narrow pathway running high above a steep ravine that drops into the Kawarau River. Chard Farm hovers, seemingly carved into the steep cliff face, and flaunts the most breathtaking vineyard location imaginable. The land, combined with a unique concentrated climate, delivers intense fruit from low-yielding vines.

Owner/winemaker Rob Hay has an instinctive interest in food and wine matching, and a belief that they should be enjoyed together. Rob produced this appropriate recipe with a good-humoured laugh, explaining that it was a very special recipe for him. In the rabbit-plagued region of Central Otago, this dish gives him 'a wonderful sense of self-sufficiency'. Rabbit cooked in and eaten with wine produced on the property – the perfect dish. **JLeC**

Rabbit with rosemary & green olives

SERVES 4

1 rabbit, jointed (or substitute chicken or duck)
1/4 cup extra virgin olive oil
2 cups Chard Farm Pinot Noir
4 cloves garlic, chopped
3 sprigs rosemary
2 tblsp plain flour
1 cup green olives, drained
2 tomatoes, skinned and diced
1 red pepper, seeds removed and sliced
sea salt and freshly ground black pepper

1 Place rabbit portions into a deep, non-metallic bowl and cover with olive oil and pinot noir. Leave to marinate overnight.

2 Next day remove rabbit portions and pat dry with paper towel. Reserve marinade. Heat oven to 180°C.

3 Heat a large heavy-based ovenproof casserole dish on oven element. Add a little oil and brown rabbit portions. Remove rabbit to one side. Add garlic and rosemary to pan and cook briefly. Stir in flour. Remove from heat and blend in pinot noir marinade.

4 Bring to the boil, stirring until thickened. Add olives, tomatoes, red pepper, salt and pepper and rabbit portions. Cover and bake in oven for 30–40 minutes.

Recipe supplied by Rob Hay, Chard Farm

Wine: Chard Farm Finla Mor Pinot Noir

Like chicken, rabbit is a meat that can be partnered by either white or red wine, depending on how it is cooked. This recipe uses a healthy dollop of Chard Farm pinot in the cooking process, so the same wine is a logical and correct accompaniment. The Farm makes at least two pinots in most vintages, and intense fruit is always a hallmark of their style. The white end of the portfolio includes an always-lively sauvignon blanc, a high-acid riesling that needs a few years of quiet time to show its best, a grunty oak-influenced pinot gris, a stylish but assertive gewürztraminer and a couple of differently styled chardonnays. They are often hard to find around the country, so it's worth getting on the mailing list. **VW**

Chard Farm

LEMON CHUTNEY

MAKES 1 LITRE

6 lemons

2 cups white wine vinegar

1/2 cup water

1 cooking apple, peeled

4 cloves garlic, crushed

2 onions, peeled and minced

good pinch saffron threads

1 tblsp horseradish

2 tblsp grated fresh ginger

2 tsp sea salt

2 cups sugar

1 Squeeze lemons and slice lemon skins into thin strips. Place lemon juice and strips into a large non-metallic bowl with vinegar and water. Cover and leave overnight.

2 Next day, tip contents of the bowl into a stainless steel preserving pan or large saucepan. Add remaining ingredients, except sugar. Bring to the boil, then gently simmer for 20–30 minutes or until lemon slices are tender.

3 Add sugar and stir over heat until dissolved. Boil briskly for 5–10 minutes until reduced to a thick but spoonable consistency. Ladle into hot sterilised jars and seal well (see mustard fruits, page 104 for sterilisation method).

4 Leave for 1 month in a cool dark place before using. Refrigerate after opening.

5 Excellent with fish or chicken and Rippon Vineyard Riesling.

Recipe created by Julie Le Clerc

WINE: RIPPON DRY RIESLING

The clean-cut, citric characters of Rippon's dry riesling need food to show their best. Julie's lemon chutney would help provide a link between the wine and a variety of dishes, from a chicken pie to grilled prawns.

Rippon Vineyard is one of the great names of the Central Otago wine scene. Sadly, Rolfe Mills died late in 2000, but his wife, Lois, remains fully committed to promoting not only their own label, but also the region as a whole. Riesling is the variety on which the company has hung its hat, but the range includes a couple of excellent variations on the pinot noir theme, elegant chardonnay, racy sauvignon blanc, a very stylish méthode traditionnelle that goes by the name of Emma, and a couple of unique wines made from exceedingly rare osteiner and gamay grapes. **VW**

RIPPON VINEYARD

Sunrise is the perfect time to view the incredible vista that is Rippon Vineyard. The rays of the new sun spread out like fingers to touch the rows of vines running down to the shores of Lake Wanaka and its small central island. A thin halo of cloud in the early morning light clings to the foothills like a necklace, and solid, purple mountains frame the whole breathtaking spectacle.

Rippon Vineyard produces excellent cool climate wines of purity, with optimum concentration of fruit. Their high acid riesling, for example, exhibits citrus, mineral, apple perfume and steely characters. High acid promotes longevity in wine. 'It's austere, punchy and hard to approach in its youth, but given four to five years it comes into its own,' says winemaker Russell Lake of this wine. 'Riesling is a noble variety in all the famous grape-growing regions of the world and I have great faith in it.' **JLeC**

189

Peregrine

A ribbon of long white cloud stretches across the land as far as the eye can see. Rugged mountains drop down to yet another stunning vineyard setting in the Kawarau Gorge, near Queenstown. Peregrine is constructed around two quaint stone cottages, some of the oldest buildings in the area. The cottages have been sympathetically restored and are used as an office, tasting room and cellar door. Delicatessen foods are also available for sale, allowing visitors to put together a picnic (or bring their own) and graze on nibbles and exuberant Peregrine wines by the lake.

Future plans include the development of a café-style eatery in the site's grand old woolshed. In keeping with the consummate style of Peregrine, this enterprise will no doubt be a winner. A full-scale winery will also be built on the estate in the not-too-distant future. **JLeC**

Smoked paprika chicken with nectarine salsa

SERVES 4

NECTARINE SALSA:

3 nectarines, stones removed

1 tblsp lemon juice

1 tblsp liquid honey

1/4 cup Peregrine Gewürztraminer

2 spring onions, finely chopped

1 tblsp grated fresh ginger

1 tsp ground cinnamon

1/4 cup slivered almonds, toasted

sea salt and freshly ground black pepper

1 Cut nectarine flesh into small dice and sprinkle with lemon juice. Mix with remaining ingredients and chill well.

SMOKED PAPRIKA CHICKEN:

4 chicken legs, drumstick separated from thigh

finely grated zest of one orange

3 cloves garlic, crushed

1 tblsp La Chinata sweet Spanish smoked paprika

1/4 tsp La Chinata hot Spanish smoked paprika

3 tblsp extra virgin olive oil

sea salt and freshly ground black pepper

1 Pre-heat oven to 180°C. Place chicken legs into an oven pan.

2 Mix remaining ingredients together to form a thick paste. Rub paste into chicken skin. Roast for 25 minutes or until juices run clear when a skewer is inserted into the thickest part of chicken.

3 Serve chicken topped with salsa.

Recipe created by Julie Le Clerc

Wine: Peregrine Gewürztraminer

Peregrine started out as a 'virtual' wine company, owning neither grapes nor a winery. Fruit was bought from local growers and made by contract winemakers in borrowed premises. Now, its own vines have been planted and a winery is on the drawing board. The label established an early name for the quality of its gewürztraminer, usually made just off-dry. The super-aromatic style suits chicken, and the link is enhanced by the ginger and cinnamon flavours in Julie's salsa.

Other impressive wines in the range include excellent pinot gris, nicely fruited riesling and approachable pinot noir. **VW**

Two Paddocks.

Two Paddocks

Peregrine

Two Paddocks

Two Paddocks is one vineyard near Queenstown dedicated entirely to premium pinot noir. A second vineyard, established near Alexandra, is christened Alex Paddock. Both vineyards are part of actor Sam Neill's family-owned enterprise, and produce powerful and distinguished hand-grown wine. The vines are low yielding and the fruit ripens slowly over a long season in the classic cool climate manner.

Stomping up to the top for a better view over the Alex Paddock vines, a blast of aromatic air assails the senses as crushed wild thyme emanates from underfoot – pure inspiration for the culinary minded! The view reveals an ingenious arrangement of bird netting, draped full length over the entire vine area instead of over individual rows. The wrappings protect the fruit from birds, of course, but this brilliant method, developed by the viticulturist, appears to be less labour intensive as well as more effective than the standard procedure. **JLeC**

Venison sausages with wild thyme gnocchi

SERVES 4

750g potatoes, peeled and roughly chopped
30g butter
1 3/4 cups plain flour
1 egg yolk
3 tblsp fresh thyme leaves
salt and pepper
350g venison sausages
1/2 cup venison glaze (reduced venison stock)
extra sprigs of thyme

1   Cook potato in boiling salted water until tender. Drain and dry, then mash and sieve potato. Beat in melted butter, then flour and egg yolk, thyme and pepper to season. Stir until dough is soft but elastic.
2   Roll into long thin sausage shapes. Cut into 2cm sections with a floury knife.
3   Drop the gnocchi in batches into a large saucepan of boiling, salted water. When cooked the gnocchi will float to the surface. Remove with a slotted spoon to a serving dish.
4   Grill sausages, slice and toss in a pan with venison glaze and gnocchi to heat. Serve immediately garnished with thyme.

Recipe created by Julie Le Clerc

Wine: Two Paddocks Neill Pinot Noir

Pinot noir and red game meat are made for one another, so venison was a logical choice for a winery that produces only pinot. Julie's dish makes good use of local herbs, but the thyme also links with the faintly herbal finish on the Two Paddocks wine.

Two Paddocks is not simply a flight of fancy for Sam Neill. Heavily involved with the local scene, he spends as much time in the vineyard as his schedule will allow, and makes a point of attending meetings of Central Otago winemakers and winery owners whenever he can. The wine is made at the Central Otago Wine Company premises, in which Sam has an interest. **VW**

Gibbston Valley Wines

VINEYARD ADDRESSES

NORTHLAND & AUCKLAND

Matakana Estate (p. 14)
568 Matakana Rd
Matakana
Ph: 09 425 0494
Fx: 09 425 0595
cellar@matakana-estate.co.nz

Heron's Flight (p. 17)
49 Sharp Rd
Matakana, RD 2
Warkworth
Ph/fx: 09 422 7915
heronfly@wk.planet.gen.nz

Kumeu River Wines (p. 19)
550 SH 16
(PO Box 24)
Kumeu
Ph: 09 412 8415
Fx: 09 412 7627
enquiries@kumeuriver.co.nz
www.kumeuriver.co.nz

Mudbrick Vineyard (p. 21)
Church Bay Rd
(PO Box 130)
Oneroa
Waiheke Island
Ph: 09 372 9050
Fx: 09 372 9051
mudbrick@ihug.co.nz
www.mudbrick.co.nz

Goldwater Estate (p. 22)
18 Causeway Rd
Putiki Bay
Waiheke Island
Ph: 09 372 7493
Fx: 09 372 6827
info@goldwaterwine.com

Matua Valley Wines (p. 26)
Waikoukou Valley Rd
Waimauku
(PO Box 100)
Kumeu
Ph: 09 411 8301
Fx: 09 411 7982
sales@matua.co.nz
www.matua.co.nz

Stonyridge Vineyard (p. 28)
80 Onetangi Rd
(PO Box 265, Ostend)
Waiheke Island
Ph: 09 372 8822
Fx: 09 372 8766
enquiries@stonyridge.co.nz
www.stonyridge.co.nz

GISBORNE & BAY OF PLENTY

Millton Vineyard (p. 34)
119 Papatu Rd
(PO Box 66)
Manutuke
Gisborne
Ph: 06 862 8680
Fx: 06 862 8869
info@millton.co.nz
www.millton.co.nz

Mills Reef Winery (p. 36)
143 Moffat Rd
Bethlehem
(PO Box 2247)
Tauranga
Ph: 07 576 8800
Fx: 07 576 8824
info@millsreef.co.nz
www.millsreef.co.nz

Morton Estate Wines (p. 37)
Main Rd
SH 2
Katikati, RD 2
(PO Box 1334, Auckland)
Ph: 09 300 5053
Fx: 09 300 5054
Winery freephone: 0800 667 866
auckland@mortonestatewines.co.nz

Matawhero Wines (p. 40)
Riverpoint Rd
Matawhero
Gisborne, RD 1
Ph: 06 868 8366
Fx: 06 867 9856

HAWKE'S BAY

Esk Valley Estate (p. 46)
Main Rd
(PO Box 111)
Bayview
Napier
Ph: 06 836 6411
Fx: 06 836 6413
enquiries@eskvalley.co.nz

Church Road Winery (p. 48)
150 Church Rd
(PO Box 7095)
Taradale
Ph: 06 844 2053
Fx: 06 844 3378
thecellardoor@montanawines.co.nz
www.montanawines.com

Crab Farm Winery (p. 52)
511 Main Rd
Bayview
Napier
Ph: 06 836 6678
Fx: 06 836 7379
info@crabfarmwinery.co.nz
www.crabfarmwinery.co.nz

Mission Estate (p. 53)
198 Church Rd
Greenmeadows
(PO Box 7043, Taradale
Napier
Ph: 06 844 2259
Fx: 06 844 6023
missionwinery@clear.net.nz

Sacred Hill Wines (p. 54)
1033 Dartmoor Rd
(James Rochford Place)
Hastings, RD 5
Napier
Ph: 06 879 8760
Fx: 06 879 4158
enquiries@sacredhill.com

Te Awa Farm Winery (p. 56)
2375 SH 50
Hastings, RD 5
Ph: 06 879 7602
Fx: 06 879 7756
winery@teawafarm.co.nz

Sileni Estates (p. 58)
2016 Maraekakaho Rd
Bridge Pa
(PO Box 2234, Stortford Lodge)
Hastings
Ph: 06 879 8768
Fx: 06 879 7187
sileni.estates@xtra.co.nz

Stonecroft (p. 61)
121 Mere Rd
Hastings, RD 5
Ph/fax: 06 879 9610
stonecroft@xtra.co.nz
www.stonecroft.co.nz

Ngatarawa Wines (p. 62)
305 Ngatarawa Rd
Hastings, RD 5
Ph: 0508 STABLES
Fx: 06 879 6675
ngatarawawines@clear.net.nz
www.ngatarawawines.co.nz

CJ Pask Winery (p. 65)
1133 Omahu Rd
(PO Box 849)
Hastings
Ph: 06 879 7906
Fx: 06 879 6428
info@cjpaskwinery.co.nz
www.cjpaskwinery.co.nz

Vidal Estate (p. 66)
913 St Aubyn St East
(PO Box 48)
Hastings
Ph: 06 876 8105
Fx: 06 876 5312
enquiries@vidalestate.co.nz

Brookfields Vineyards (p. 69)
376 Brookfields Rd
Meeanee
(PO Box 7174, Taradale)
Napier
Ph: 06 834 4615
Fx: 06 834 4622
brookfields.vineyards@xtra.co.nz

Trinity Hill (p. 72)
2396 SH 50
(PO Box 2150, Stortford Lodge)
Hastings, RD 5
Ph: 06 879 7778
Fx: 06 879 7770
trinityhill@xtra.co.nz
www.trinityhillwines.co.nz

Clearview Estate Winery (p. 74)
194 Clifton Rd
Te Awanga
Hastings, RD 2
Ph: 06 875 0150
Fx: 06 875 1258
wine@clearviewestate.co.nz
www.clearviewestate.co.nz

WAIRARAPA

Martinborough Vineyard (p. 80)
Princess St
(PO Box 85)
Martinborough
Ph: 06 306 9955
Fx: 06 306 9217
winery@mvwine.co.nz
www.martinborough-vineyard.co.nz

Palliser Estate Wines of Martinborough (p. 82)
Kitchener St
(PO Box 110)
Martinborough
Ph: 06 306 9019
Fx: 06 306 9946
palliser@palliser.co.nz
www.palliser.co.nz

Winslow Wines (p. 85)
Princess St
(PO Box 64)
Martinborough
Ph: 06 306 9648
Fx: 06 306 9271
winwine@xtra.co.nz
www.winslow.co.nz

Margrain Vineyard (p. 86)
Cnr Ponatahi and Huangarua Rds
(PO Box 97)
Martinborough
Ph: 06 306 9292
Fx: 06 306 9297
margrain@xtra.co.nz
www.margrainvineyard.co.nz

Nga Waka Vineyard (p. 89)
Kitchener St
(PO Box 128)
Martinborough
Ph/fax: 06 306 9832
ngawaka@voyager.co.nz
www.nzwine.com/ngawaka

Te Kairanga Wines (p. 91)
Martins Rd
(PO Box 52)
Martinborough
Ph: 06 306 9122
Fx: 06 306 9322
tekairanga@xtra.co.nz
www.tkwine.co.nz

Gladstone Vineyard (p. 92)
Gladstone Rd
Carterton, RD 2
Ph: 06 379 8563
Fx: 06 379 8564
wines@gladstone.co.nz
www.gladstone.co.nz

Ata Rangi (p. 96)
Puruatanga Rd
(PO Box 43)
Martinborough
Ph: 06 306 9570
Fx: 06 306 9523
wines@atarangi.co.nz

Dry River Wines (p. 98)
Puruatanga Rd
(PO Box 72)
Martinborough
Ph: 06 306 9388
Fx: 06 306 9275

NELSON

Denton Winery (p. 104)
Awa Awa Rd, off Marriages Rd
Ruby Bay
Nelson
Ph/fax: 03 540 3555
denton.winery@xtra.co.nz

Moutere Hills Vineyard (p. 107)
Eggers Rd,
Sunrise Valley
Upper Moutere, RD 1
Nelson
Ph/fax: 03 543 2288
mouterehills@actrix.co.nz

Glover's Vineyard (p. 108)
Gardner Valley Rd
Upper Moutere, RD 1
Nelson
Ph/fax: 03 543 2698
info@glovers-vineyard.co.nz
www.glovers-vineyard.co.nz

Seifried Estate (p. 111)
Redwood Rd
Appleby
(PO Box 7020)
Nelson
Ph: 03 544 5599
Fx: 03 544 5522
wines@seifried.co.nz
www.seifried.co.nz

Neudorf Vineyards (p. 112)
Neudorf Rd
Upper Moutere, RD 2
Nelson
Ph: 03 543 2643
Fx: 03 543 2955
neudorf@neudorf.co.nz
www.neudorf.co.nz

BLENHEIM & MARLBOROUGH

Seresin Estate (p. 118)
Bedford Rd
Renwick, RD 1
Blenheim
Ph: 03 572 9408
Fx: 03 572 9850
info@seresin.co.nz
www.seresin.co.nz

Cellier Le Brun (p. 120)
169 Terrace Rd
(PO Box 33)
Renwick
Marlborough
Ph: 03 572 8859
Fx: 03 572 8814
sales@lebrun.co.nz
www.lebrun.co.nz

Hunter's Wines (p. 125)
Rapaura Rd
(PO Box 839)
Blenheim
Ph: 03 572 8489
Fx: 03 572 8457

hunters@voyager.co.nz
www.hunters.co.nz

**Allan Scott Wines
& Estates** (p. 126)
Jackson's Rd
Blenheim, RD 3
Ph: 03 572 9054
Fx: 03 572 9053
scott.wines@xtra.co.nz
www.allanscott.com

Highfield Estate (p. 127)
Brookby Rd
Omaka Valley
Blenheim, RD 2
Ph: 03 572 9244
Fx: 03 572 9257
wine@highfield.co.nz
www.highfield.co.nz

Vavasour Wines (p. 128)
Redwood Pass
Awatere Valley
(PO Box 72)
Seddon
Marlborough
Ph: 03 575 7481
Fx: 03 575 7240
vavasour@vavasour.com
www.vavasour.com

**Framingham Wine
Company** (p. 130)
Conders Bend Rd
(PO Box 37, Renwick)
Marlborough
Ph: 03 572 8884
Fx: 03 572 9884
framwine@voyager.co.nz
www.framingham.co.nz

Fromm Winery (p. 133)
Godfrey Rd
Blenheim, RD 2
Ph: 03 572 9355
Fx: 03 572 9366
LaStrada@frommwineries.com
www.frommwineries.com

**Montana Brancott
Winery** (p. 135)
Main Rd South
SH 1
Riverlands
(PO Box 331)
Blenheim
Ph: 03 578 2099
Fx: 03 578 0463
marlwinery@montanawines.co.nz
www.montanawines.com

Wither Hills Vineyard (p. 136)
New Renwick Rd
Blenheim, RD 2
(58 Victoria Ave, Remuera, Auckland)
Ph/fax: 09 378 0857
winery@witherhills.co.nz
www.witherhills.co.nz

Cloudy Bay (p. 138)
Jackson's Rd
(PO Box 376)
Blenheim
Ph: 03 520 9140
Fx: 03 520 9040
info@cloudybay.co.nz
www.cloudybay.co.nz

Mount Riley (p. 141)
Cnr Rapaura Rd and SH 6
(PO Box 5012, Springlands)
Blenheim
Ph: 09 489 1042
Fx: 09 489 4502
steve.mountriley@xtra.co.nz

Wairau River Wines (p. 142)
Cnr SH 6 & Rapaura Rd
(Giffords Rd)
Blenheim, RD 3
Ph: 03 572 9800
Fx: 03 572 9885
office@WairauRiverWines.com
www.WairauRiverWines.com

Spy Valley Wines (p. 147)
Waihopai Valley Rd
Marlborough, RD 6
Ph: 03 572 9840
Fx: 03 572 9830
b.agibbs@xtra.co.nz

Grove Mill (p. 148)
Waihopai Valley Rd
(PO Box 67, Renwick)
Marlborough
Ph: 03 572 8200
Fx: 03 572 8211
info@grovemill.co.nz

CANTERBURY & WAIPARA

Kaituna Valley (p. 155)
230 Kaituna Valley Rd
Christchurch, RD 2
Ph: 03 329 0110
Fx: 03 329 0113
kaituna.valley@xtra.co.nz

Giesen Wine Estate (p. 156)
Burnham School Rd
(PO Box 11 066)
Burnham

Christchurch
Ph 03 347 6729
Fx 03 347 6450
info@giesen.co.nz
www.giesen.co.nz

St Helena Wine Estate (p. 158)
Coutts Island Rd
(PO Box 1)
Belfast
Christchurch
Ph 03 323 8202
Fx 03 323 8252
sthelena@xtra.co.nz

Waipara West (p. 162)
376 Ram Paddock Rd
Amberley, RD 2
Ph: 03 314 8699
Fx: 03 314 8692
waiparawest@xtra.co.nz
waiparawest.com

**Canterbury House
Winery** (p. 164)
780 Glasnevin Rd
Waipara
(PO Box 111)
Amberley
Ph: 03 314 6900
Fx: 03 314 6905
canterburyhouse@attglobal.net
www.canterburyhouse.com

Fiddler's Green (p. 165)
Georges Rd
Waipara
(PO Box 81)
Amberley
Ph: 03 314 6979
Fx: 03 314 6978
fiddler@xtra.co.nz

Pegasus Bay (p. 167)
Stockgrove Rd
Amberley, RD 2
Ph/fax: 03 314 6869
info@pegasusbay.com
www.pegasusbay.com

Muddy Water Fine Wines (p. 168)
424 Omihi Rd
(PO Box 36 011)
Waipara
Ph: 03 377 7123
Fx: 03 377 7130
wine@muddywater.co.nz
www.muddywater.co.nz

Mountford Vineyard (p. 172)
434 Omihi Rd
Waipara

Ph: 03 314 6819
Fx: 03 314 6820
wl@mountfordvineyard.co.nz
www.mountfordvineyard.co.nz

Waipara Springs Wine (p. 174)
409 Omihi Rd
(PO Box 17)
Waipara
Ph/fax: 03 314 6777
www.wineonline.co.nz/
waiparasprings

CENTRAL OTAGO

Gibbston Valley Wines (p. 180)
Main Queenstown-Cromwell
Highway
Queenstown, RD 1
Ph: 03 442 6910
Fx: 03 442 6909
gvwines.co.nz
www.gvwines.co.nz

Felton Road (p. 183)
Felton Rd
Bannockburn
Central Otago
Ph: 03 445 0885
Fx: 03 445 0881
wines@FeltonRoad.com
www.FeltonRoad.com

Chard Farm (p. 184)
Chard Rd
Queenstown, RD 1
Ph: 03 442 6110
Fx: 03 441 8400
sales@chardfarm.co.nz
www.chardfarm.co.nz

Rippon Vineyard (p. 189)
Mount Aspiring Rd
(PO Box 175)
Lake Wanaka
Ph: 03 443 8084
Fx: 03 443 8034
rippon@xtra.co.nz
www.rippon.co.nz

Peregrine (p. 190)
Kawarau Gorge Rd
Queenstown, RD 1
Ph: 03 442 4000
Fx: 03 442 4038
peregrine@xtra.co.nz
www.peregrinewines.co.nz

Two Paddocks (p. 194)
For wine sales:
Ph: 03 442 4283
Fx: 03 441 1123
twopaddocks@xtra.co.nz